TOSEL®

READING SERIES

READING
HIGH JUNIOR
2

ITC International TOSEL Committee

CONTENTS

About TOSEL®

TOSEL (Test of Skills in the English Language) was developed to meet the demand for a more effective assessment of English as a foreign language for learners from specific cultural settings.

TOSEL evaluates and certifies the proficiency levels of English learners, from the age of 4 through adulthood, along with academic and job performance results.

Background

- Other English tests are ineffective in accurately measuring individual abilities
- Overuse of US-dominated testing systems in diverse cultural and educational contexts in the global English language learning market

Functions & Usage

- Assessment is categorized into 7 levels
- Used as a qualification for academic excellence for school admissions
- Used as a test to assess the English proficiency in the corporate and public sectors

Goals

- Create an effective tool for assessing and evaluating the English skills of English language learners
- Implement efficient and accessible testing systems and methods
- Provide constructive and developmental English education guidance

TOSEL® Strength

LEVELED ASSESSMENTS

An established English test system fit for seven different levels according to learners' cognitive development

ACCURATE DIAGNOSIS

A systematic and scientific diagnosis of learners' English proficiency

EXTENSIVE MATERIALS

Supplementary materials to help learners in an EFL environment to prepare for TOSEL and improve their proficiency

SUFFICIENT DATA

Content for each level developed by using data accumulated from more than 2,000,000 TOSEL test takers delegated at 15,000 schools and academies

CLASSIFIED AREAS OF INTELLIGENCE

Content designed to foster and expand the strengths of each student, categorized by the eight areas of intelligence

CONTINUITY

A complete course of English education ranging from kindergarten, elementary school, middle school, high schoool, and up to adults.

HIGH RELIABILITY

A high reliability level (Cronbach's alpha: .904 for elementary school students / .864 for university students) proven by several studies (Oxford University / Modern Language Journal)

SYSTEMATIC & EFFECTIVE ENGLISH EDUCATION

Accurate diagnosis and extensive materials which provide a step-by-step development in English learning, according to the quality of each learner's ability

TOSEL® Level Chart

Seven Separate Assessments

TOSEL divides the test into seven stages, by considering the test takers' cognitive levels, according to different ages. Unlike other assessments based on only one level, TOSEL includes separate assessments for preschool, elementary school, middle school, high school students, and for adults, which also includes both professionals and college students.

TOSEL's reporting system highlights the strengths and weaknesses of each test taker and suggests areas for further development.

COCOON

Suitable for children aged 4-6 (pre-schoolers)

The first step in the TOSEL system, the test is composed of colorful designs and interesting questions to interest young learners and to put them at ease.

Pre-STARTER

Suitable for children aged 7-8 (1st-2nd grades of elementary school)

Evaluates the ability to comprehend simple vocabulary, conversations, and sentences.

STARTER

Suitable for children aged 9-10 (3rd-4th grades of elementary school)

Evaluates the ability to comprehend short sentences and conversations related to everyday situations or topics.

BASIC

Suitable for children aged 11-12 (5th–6th grades of elementary school)

Evaluates the ability to communicate about personal information, daily activities, future plans, and past experiences in written and spoken language.

JUNIOR

Suitable for middle school students

Evaluates the ability to comprehend short paragraphs, practical texts, and speech covering general topics and to participate in simple daily conversations.

HIGH JUNIOR

Suitable for high school students

Evaluates the ability to use English fluently, accurately, and effectively on a wide range of social and academic subjects, as well as the ability to use sentences with a variety of complex structures.

ADVANCED

Suitable for university students and adults

Evaluates the ability to use practical English required for a job or work environment, as well as the ability to use and understand English at the university level.

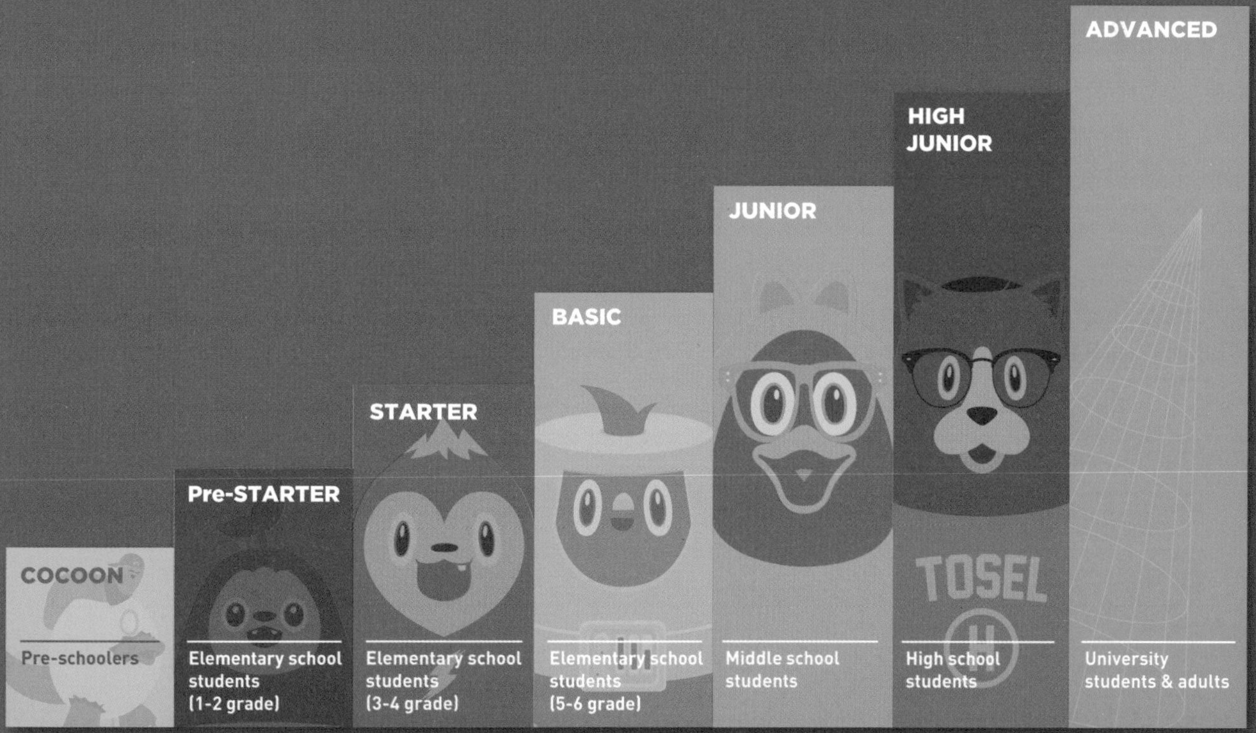

Evaluation

Assessing the Four Skills

TOSEL evaluates the four language skills: reading, listening, speaking and writing, through indirect and direct assessment items.

This system of evaluation is part of a concerted effort to break away from materials geared solely toward grammar and reading-oriented education.

TOSEL Test Information

Level	Score	Grade	Section	
			Section I Listening & Speaking	Section II Reading & Writing
COCOON	100		15 Questions / 15 min	15 Questions / 15 min
Pre-STARTER	100		15 Questions / 15 min	20 Questions / 25 min
STARTER	100		20 Questions / 15 min	20 Questions / 25 min
BASIC	100	1-10	30 Questions / 20 min	30 Questions / 30 min
JUNIOR	100		30 Questions / 20 min	30 Questions / 30 min
HIGH JUNIOR	100		30 Questions / 25 min	35 Questions / 35 min
ADVANCED	990		70 Questions / 45 min	70 Questions / 55 min

Certificates

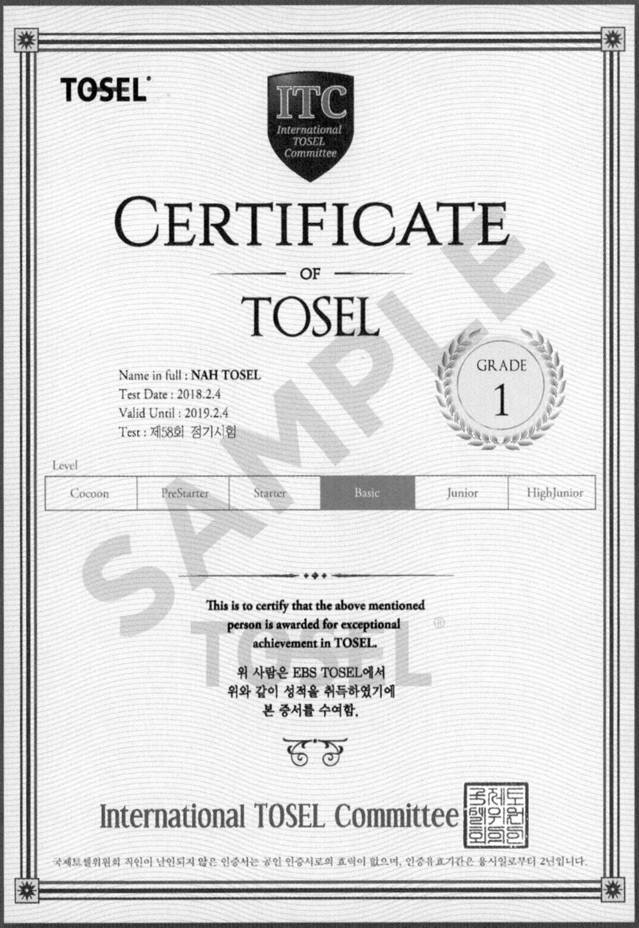

TOSEL Certificate

The International TOSEL Committee officially evaluates and certifies the level of English proficiency of English learners from the age of 4 to adults.

Certified by

Mar. 2010	Korea University
Dec. 2009	The Korean Society of Speech Science
Dec. 2009	The Korea Association of Foreign Language Education
Nov. 2009	The Applied Linguistics Association of Korea
Oct. 2009	The Pan Korea English Teachers Association

CHAPTER 1

Health

Teacher's Book
p.112

UNIT 1

Health Literacy

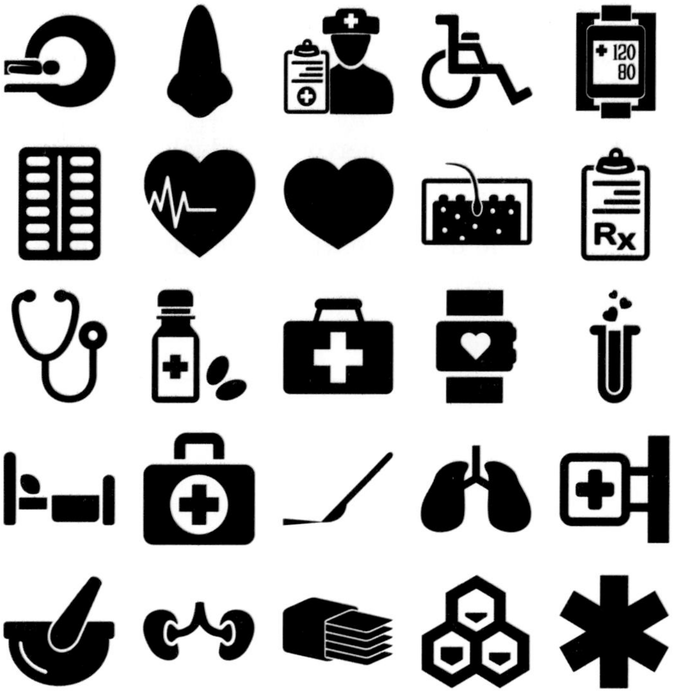

Where would you most likely see these signs?
Do you know what they mean?

Health Literacy

Imagine the following scenario. David is told by his doctor that he has tested positive for diabetes. Mistakenly thinking that "testing positive" means he does not have the disease, David is relieved. Or imagine that Lei cannot understand the symbols on the signs at a hospital. Too embarrassed to ask for directions, she leaves the hospital and misses her appointment. These two cases are examples of low health literacy, a problem that is receiving increasing recognition in the medical community.

Broadly speaking, health literacy is the extent to which an individual is able to access and understand health-related information and services. The concept includes issues related to cultural knowledge, language differences, math skills, and communication skills. Health literacy is not just about understanding instructions. It also has to do with patients' ability to figure out what questions they need to ask as well as their capacity to make decisions about their health.

In the past, low health literacy was considered individuals' problem. Now it is generally acknowledged that health literacy is a societal concern. Health care providers, the government, and the education system need to do a better job of helping people to understand crucial information that could mark the difference between life and death.

New Words

scenario *n* an imagined series of events	diabetes *n* a serious disease related to blood sugar
relieved *adj* no longer anxious	literacy *n* the ability to read
societal *adj* related to people in society	health care providers *n* medical workers

Part A. Picture Description

1.

She was worried before. Now she seems ________.

(A) frantic
(B) ecstatic
(C) relieved
(D) boastful

2.

As picture B shows, this is a major ________ issue.

(A) solo
(B) societal
(C) scientific
(D) scholarly

Part B. Sentence Completion

3. ________, the term "health" refers to a state of wellbeing.

(A) Broad speaking
(B) Broadly speaking
(C) To speak of it broad
(D) To be spoken broadly

4. Sewing used to be ________ an essential skill. Now fewer people know how to do it.

(A) to consider
(B) considered
(C) considering
(D) we considered

Part C. Practical Reading Comprehension

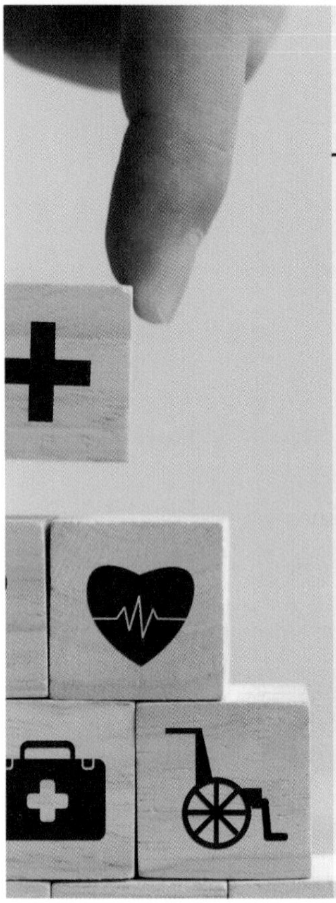

The way you communicate with your patients will help with their care. Your communication style is a part of health literacy.

To make health information easier to understand, do the following:

- Limit how many messages you give.
- Use simple language. Medical terms are usually too difficult for most people to understand.
- Practice respectful intercultural speech.
- Focus on action. What do you need your patients to do?
- Check for understanding. Get your patients to say what you told them in their own words.
- Use pictures to help people to understand.
- Use an interpreter or translator who has medical training. Not every medical issue can be put into simple words.

5. For whom is this information most likely written?

(A) hospital patients
(B) science teachers
(C) health care workers
(D) parents of sick children

6. Which of the following is mentioned as a tip?

(A) utilizing images
(B) becoming bilingual
(C) never using medical language
(D) repeating the message three times

Part D. General Reading Comprehension

Imagine the following scenario. David is told by his doctor that he has tested positive for diabetes. Mistakenly thinking that "testing positive" means he does not have the disease, David is relieved. Or imagine that Lei cannot understand the symbols on the signs at a hospital. Too embarrassed to ask for directions, she leaves the hospital and misses her appointment. These two cases are examples of low health literacy, a problem that is receiving increasing recognition in the medical community.

Broadly speaking, health literacy is the extent to which an individual is able to access and understand health-related information and services. The concept includes issues related to cultural knowledge, language differences, math skills, and communication skills. Health literacy is not just about understanding instructions. It also has to do with patients' ability to figure out what questions they need to ask as well as their capacity to make decisions about their health.

In the past, low health literacy was considered individuals' problem. Now it is generally acknowledged that health literacy is a societal concern. Health care providers, the government, and the education system need to do a better job of helping people to understand crucial information that could mark the difference between life and death.

7. What is the main idea of the passage?

(A) Computers can be used to help patients.
(B) Low health literacy is a recognized problem.
(C) Errors by surgeons are increasing in number.
(D) People dislike asking their doctors questions.

8. In the examples, what mistake does David make?

(A) leaving a hospital without paying a bill
(B) going to his appointment at the wrong time
(C) misunderstanding the meaning of a medical term
(D) forgetting to tell his doctor about some symptoms

9. Which is NOT listed as a part of health literacy?

(A) math skills
(B) physical abilities
(C) cultural knowledge
(D) language differences

10. Which statement would the writer most likely agree with?

(A) Health literacy should be taught in schools.
(B) Schools used to be better at teaching about health.
(C) Health literacy should no longer be taught in schools.
(D) Schools should reduce time for physical education classes.

Listening Practice

Listen and write.

MP3 HJ2-1

Health Literacy

Imagine the following 1 __________. David is told by his doctor that he has tested positive for 2 __________. Mistakenly thinking that "testing positive" means he does not have the disease, David is 3 __________. Or imagine that Lei cannot understand the symbols on the signs at a hospital. Too embarrassed to ask for directions, she leaves the hospital and misses her appointment. These two cases are examples of low health 4 __________, a problem that is receiving increasing recognition in the medical community.

Broadly speaking, health literacy is the extent to which an individual is able to access and understand health-related information and services. The concept includes issues related to cultural knowledge, language differences, math skills, and communication skills. Health literacy is not just about understanding instructions. It also has to do with patients' ability to figure out what questions they need to ask as well as their capacity to make decisions about their health. In the past, low health literacy was considered individuals' problem. Now it is generally acknowledged that health literacy is a 5 __________ concern. Health care 6 __________, the government, and the education system need to do a better job of helping people to understand crucial information that could mark the difference between life and death.

Word Bank

scenario	Literacy	diabeetees
societal	sociedal	senario
probiders	releved	relieved
diabetes	providers	literacy

Listen. Pause. Say each sentence.

MP3 HJ2-1G

Writing Practice

Write the words.

1 ________ *n* an imagined series of events	2 ________ *n* a serious disease related to blood sugar
3 ________ *adj* no longer anxious	4 ________ *n* the ability to read
5 ________ *adj* related to people in society	6 ________ *n* medical workers

Write the words in each blank.

Summary

Low health ________________ is receiving increasing ________________ as a societal concern. Health care providers, the ________________, and the education system should work hard to solve the problems related to ________________ health literacy.

Word Puzzle

Complete the word puzzle.

Across

4 an imagined series of events

5 a serious disease related to blood sugar

Down

1 the ability to read

2 medical workers

3 no longer anxious

4 related to people in society

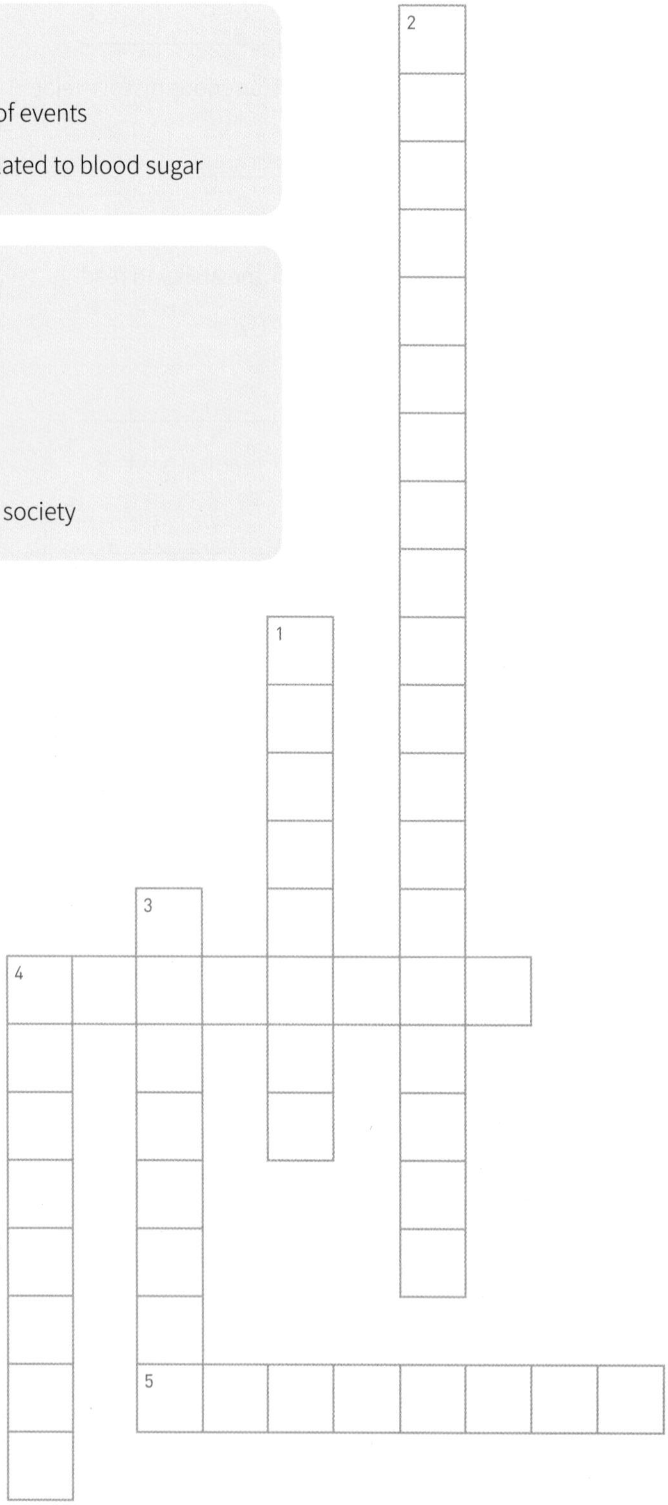

Teacher's Book p.117

UNIT 2

Yoga

Have you tried yoga?
What do you think the benefits of yoga might be?

Virtually everyone knows that yoga can help increase flexibility. However, there are numerous other advantages to this ancient practice. These comprise both physical and mental improvements.

The physical benefits of yoga include better muscle strength, a faster metabolism, cardiovascular health, and protection against injuries. Yoga can also improve the breathing of those who practice it. In one research study, college students took a 15-week yoga class. By the end of the course, participants had increased their vital capacity by a statistically significant amount. Vital capacity measures how much air a person can breathe out of their lungs at one time, and is an important way to see lung function.

In addition to the physical rewards, many mental benefits of yoga include better mental clarity, improved awareness of how one's body works, enhanced concentration, a sense of relaxation, and stress relief. Yoga can also help people with anxiety. In one study of 64 women who suffered from post-traumatic stress disorder (a condition of severe anxiety after trauma), more than half had far fewer symptoms of the condition after two and a half months of yoga.

In short, many activities can enhance either physical or mental health. However, for anyone looking to do both at the same time, they need look no further than yoga.

New Words

virtually everyone almost everyone	metabolism *n* chemical reactions in your body related to burning calories
cardiovascular *adj* related to the heart and blood vessels	statistically significant having a value in science meaning that random chance is not a likely explanation
traumatic *adj* deeply disturbing	enhance *v* improve

10 minutes

Part A. Picture Description

1.

Being on a tiny stage is ________ for the elephant.

(A) normal
(B) hilarious
(C) traumatic
(D) enjoyable

2.

It seems this medicine has ________ his wellbeing.

(A) enhanced
(B) destroyed
(C) worsened
(D) threatened

Part B. Sentence Completion

3. The physical benefits of this exercise ________ feeling stronger and being flexible.

(A) include
(B) includes
(C) would be include
(D) would have include

4. This test measures ________ in the first half of the semester.

(A) how much you learned
(B) how much did you learn
(C) much how did you learn
(D) much of how you had learn

Unusual Types of
Yoga Classes

Goat Yoga
- started in a woman's barn
- involves yoga with live goats
- goats jump around the participants, and even on top of them

Tantrum Yoga
- the intent is to release stress
- participants yell and stomp their feet
- people feel calm afterwards

Aerial Yoga
- participants do yoga in soft cloth hammocks
- the hammocks are held 1 meter above the ground
- participants gain a lot of muscle trying to keep their balance

Acroyoga
- for couples to do together
- combines yoga, acrobatics, and Thai massage
- lunar type (focuses more on massage)/ solar type (more advanced acrobatics)

5. In which type is rope netting required?

(A) goat yoga
(B) tantrum yoga
(C) aerial yoga
(D) acroyoga

6. Which of the following is true?

(A) Tantrum yoga involves shouting.
(B) Goat yoga began in a farmer's field.
(C) Acroyoga blends agriculture and yoga.
(D) People are in trees when they do aerial yoga.

Part D. General Reading Comprehension

Virtually everyone knows that yoga can help increase flexibility. However, there are numerous other advantages to this ancient practice. These comprise both physical and mental improvements.

The physical benefits of yoga include better muscle strength, a faster metabolism, cardiovascular health, and protection against injuries. Yoga can also improve the breathing of those who practice it. In one research study, college students took a 15-week yoga class. By the end of the course, participants had increased their vital capacity by a statistically significant amount. Vital capacity measures how much air a person can breathe out of their lungs at one time, and is an important way to see lung function.

In addition to the physical rewards, many mental benefits of yoga include better mental clarity, improved awareness of how one's body works, enhanced concentration, a sense of relaxation, and stress relief. Yoga can also help people with anxiety. In one study of 64 women who suffered from post-traumatic stress disorder (a condition of severe anxiety after trauma), more than half had far fewer symptoms of the condition after two and a half months of yoga.

In short, many activities can enhance either physical or mental health. However, for anyone looking to do both at the same time, they need look no further than yoga.

7. Which would be the best title for the passage?
   (A) How to Get Started in Yoga
   (B) The Physical and Mental Advantages of Yoga
   (C) Modern Updates to the Ancient Practice of Yoga
   (D) Surprising Ways in Which Yoga Can Injure People

8. According to the passage, what happened to students after a 15-week yoga class?
   (A) They had better lung capacity.
   (B) They had difficulties breathing.
   (C) They had learned to teach yoga.
   (D) They had slowed their metabolism.

9. Which benefit of yoga is listed?
   (A) thinner legs
   (B) smarter babies
   (C) enhanced hearing
   (D) better concentration

10. According to the passage, what happened to 64 women with post-traumatic health disorder?
   (A) Over 50% had fewer symptoms after 2.5 months.
   (B) A third reduced their symptoms by 2.5% in a month.
   (C) Just under 50% had more symptoms after 2.5 months.
   (D) Half saw a 75% reduction in symptoms after three months.

Listening Practice

Listen and write.

MP3 HJ2-2

Yoga

1 ________ everyone knows that yoga can help increase flexibility. However, there are numerous other advantages to this ancient practice. These comprise both physical and mental improvements.

The physical benefits of yoga include better muscle strength, a faster 2 ________, 3 ________ health, and protection against injuries. Yoga can also improve the breathing of those who practice it. In one research study, college students took a 15-week yoga class. By the end of the course, participants had increased their vital capacity by a statistically 4 ________ amount. Vital capacity measures how much air a person can breathe out of their lungs at one time, and is an important way to see lung function.

In addition to the physical rewards, many mental benefits of yoga include better mental clarity, improved awareness of how one's body works, enhanced concentration, a sense of relaxation, and stress relief. Yoga can also help people with anxiety. In one study of 64 women who suffered from post- 5 ________ stress disorder (a condition of severe anxiety after trauma), more than half had far fewer symptoms of the condition after two and a half months of yoga.

In short, many activities can 6 ________ either physical or mental health. However, for anyone looking to do both at the same time, they need look no further than yoga.

Word Bank

Virtually	dramatic	significant
inhance	cardiovascular	significent
virtually	metabolims	enhance
traumatic	cardiobascular	metabolism

Listen. Pause. Say each sentence.

MP3 HJ2-2G

Writing Practice

Write the words.

1 ________________ almost everyone	2 ________________ *n* chemical reactions in your body related to burning calories
3 ________________ *adj* related to the heart and blood vessels	4 ________________ having a value in science meaning that random chance is not a likely explanation
5 ________________ *adj* deeply disturbing	6 ________________ *v* improve

Write the words in each blank.

Summary

There are ________________ physical and ________________ advantages of yoga. Benefits include better ________________ strength and mental clarity. Therefore, people who want to ________________ both physical and mental health need to look no further than yoga.

Word Puzzle

Complete the word puzzle.

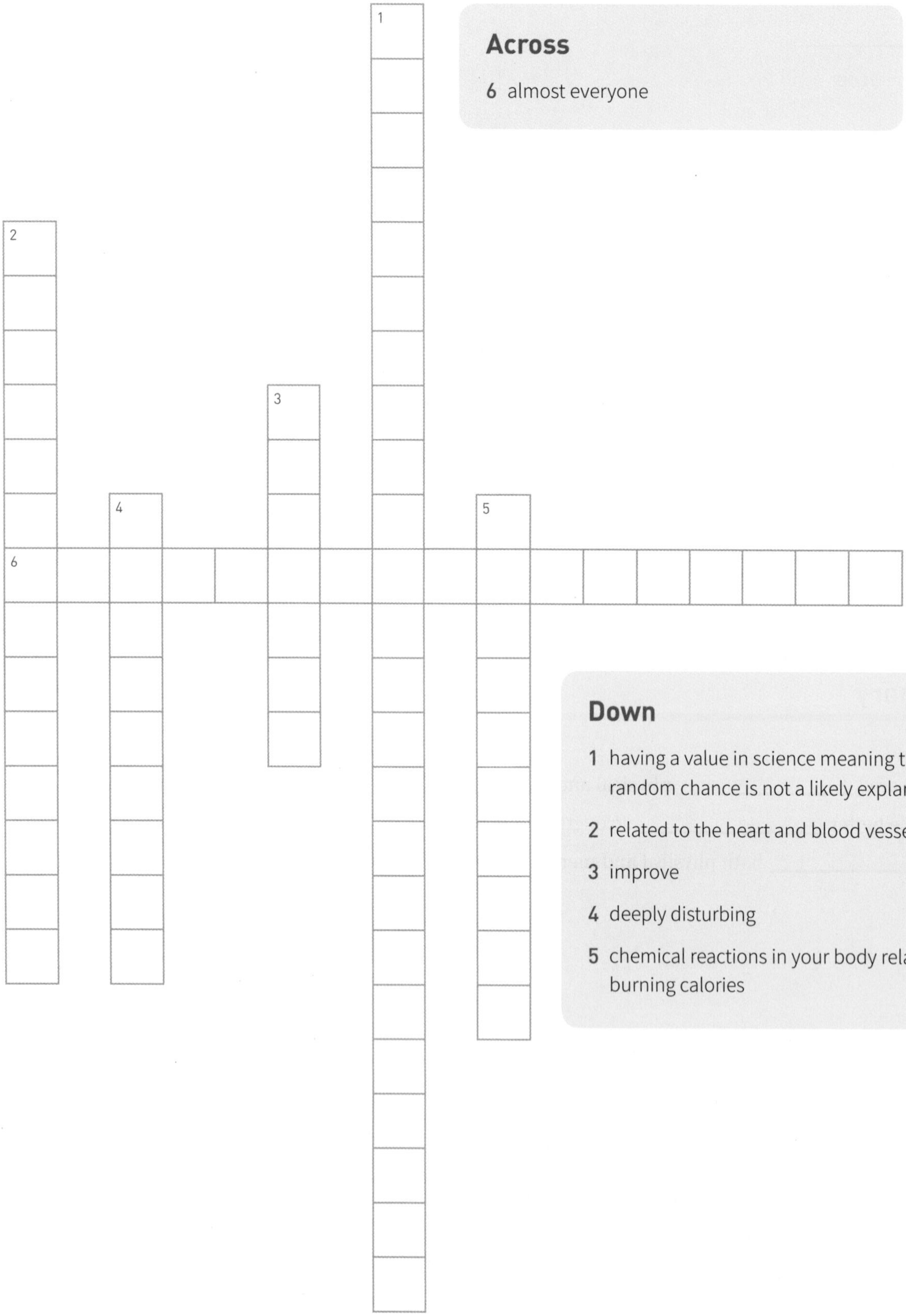

Across

6 almost everyone

Down

1 having a value in science meaning that random chance is not a likely explanation

2 related to the heart and blood vessels

3 improve

4 deeply disturbing

5 chemical reactions in your body related to burning calories

Teacher's Book
p.123

UNIT 3

Digital Eye Strain

When you look at a screen for a long time,
do your eyes ever feel tired?

UNIT 3 Digital Eye Strain

With the rise of digital screens, questions have arisen about possible strain on the eyes. Luckily, research has provided some clarity on so-called digital eye strain, as well as some advice on how to handle it.

First, those worried that the blue light in LED screens is a major cause of digital eye strain can probably worry less. There is not enough evidence to suggest that blue light itself is a cause of strained eyes. In fact, UK advertising officials banned an advertisement on blue light-blocking lenses, as the ad's claims that the eyewear could protect against eye strain, tiredness, and damage to the eye could not be supported.

However, anyone who has used a computer or mobile device for a long time has likely noticed their eyes feeling some strain. Part of this comes from staring too long at one place without blinking. It is also likely that the screen is too bright. Individuals wishing to combat eye strain can try using the 20-20-20 rule. This means that every 20 minutes, individuals should look at a distance 20 feet away for 20 seconds. They can also reduce the brightness of their screens and use fake tears or a humidifier. Until digital screens are modified, taking measures to reduce digital eye strain can help.

New Words

strain *n* tension	eyewear *n* glasses or sunglasses
blink *v* close both eyes at the same time	combat *v* fight against
humidifier *n* a device to make the air more moist	modify *v* change

Part A. Picture Description

1.

Alexi has put ________ on his back.

(A) strain
(B) a box
(C) weights
(D) a carrier

2.

Fatima ________ as our family photo was taken.

(A) winked
(B) blinked
(C) ran away
(D) sat down

Part B. Sentence Completion

3. In your application, you may not use pictures that have been ________ in any way.

(A) modify
(B) modifier
(C) modified
(D) modifying

4. There is not enough ________ to suggest that your dog is the source of your allergies.

(A) evidence
(B) evidences
(C) of evidence
(D) of it evidence

Remember This Advice When You're at Home or in the Lab

1. Make sure the light in the room is brighter than your computer monitor. If you're the first student in the lab, open the blinds.
2. Position your monitor so it is about 0.6 meters away from you.
3. If the air in the room is dry, turn on the lab's humidifier to keep your eyes moist.
4. Reduce glare on your monitor and in the room. At home, put a matte screen over your monitor. Ask your family if you can paint walls in a matte paint (and aim to make them a darker color than white).
5. Take frequent breaks from sitting in front of your computer. Many students only take two 15-minute breaks in a study day. This is not enough.

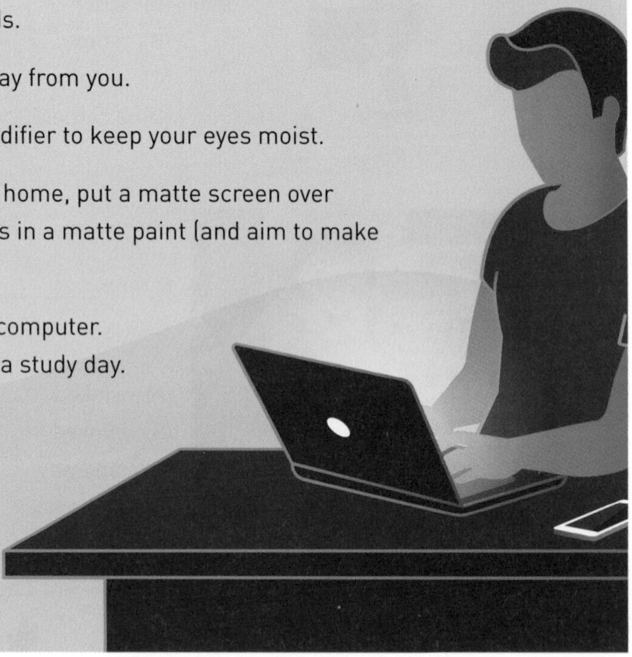

5. Where would this notice most likely be posted?

(A) in a company office
(B) in a store for electronics
(C) in a school computer lab
(D) in a magazine article about cyberbullying

6. Which of the following is NOT a given tip?

(A) Cover your monitor with a matte screen.
(B) Use the room's humidifier to help your eyes.
(C) Put your monitor at least half a meter away from you.
(D) Take just two fifteen-minute breaks in your study day.

Part D. General Reading Comprehension

With the rise of digital screens, questions have arisen about possible strain on the eyes. Luckily, research has provided some clarity on so-called digital eye strain, as well as some advice on how to handle it. First, those worried that the blue light in LED screens is a major cause of digital eye strain can probably worry less. There is not enough evidence to suggest that blue light itself is a cause of strained eyes. In fact, UK advertising officials banned an advertisement on blue light-blocking lenses, as the ad's claims that the eyewear could protect against eye strain, tiredness, and damage to the eye could not be supported. However, anyone who has used a computer or mobile device for a long time has likely noticed their eyes feeling some strain. Part of this comes from staring too long at one place without blinking. It is also likely that the screen is too bright. Individuals wishing to combat eye strain can try using the 20-20-20 rule. This means that every 20 minutes, individuals should look at a distance 20 feet away for 20 seconds. They can also reduce the brightness of their screens and use fake tears or a humidifier. Until digital screens are modified, taking measures to reduce digital eye strain can help.

7. What would be the best title for the passage?

(A) Digital Eye Strain: Clarity and Tips
(B) Eye Dryness: Prevention and Cures
(C) Digital Technologies: Optical Recognition
(D) Eye Problems: Why LED Screens Are Killing Us

8. According to the passage, why was a UK ad for blue light-blocking lenses banned?

(A) It was considered inappropriate for children.
(B) There were too many similar ads already on TV.
(C) It included blue emissions that could harm people.
(D) There was a lack of evidence to support its claims.

9. What cause of eye strain is mentioned?

(A) not blinking
(B) reading in the dark
(C) looking at small numbers
(D) sitting too close to a screen

10. Which tip is NOT recommended in the passage?

(A) Put fake tears in your eyes.
(B) Wear a cooling pack over your eyes.
(C) Look at a far distance for 20 seconds.
(D) Reduce the brightness of your screen.

Listening Practice

Listen and write.

MP3 HJ2-3

Digital Eye Strain

With the rise of digital screens, questions have arisen about possible strain on the eyes. Luckily, research has provided some clarity on so-called digital eye 1 ________, as well as some advice on how to handle it.

First, those worried that the blue light in LED screens is a major cause of digital eye strain can probably worry less. There is not enough evidence to suggest that blue light itself is a cause of strained eyes. In fact, UK advertising officials banned an advertisement on blue light-blocking lenses, as the ad's claims that the 2 ________ could protect against eye strain, tiredness, and damage to the eye could not be supported.

However, anyone who has used a computer or mobile device for a long time has likely noticed their eyes feeling some strain. Part of this comes from staring too long at one place without 3 ________. It is also likely that the screen is too bright. Individuals wishing to 4 ________ eye strain can try using the 20-20-20 rule. This means that every 20 minutes, individuals should look at a distance 20 feet away for 20 seconds. They can also reduce the brightness of their screens and use fake tears or a 5 ________. Until digital screens are 6 ________, taking measures to reduce digital eye strain can help.

Word Bank

kombat	strane	modified
strain	blinking	modyfied
humidifier	eyewears	blink in
eyewear	hummidifier	combat

Listen. Pause. Say each sentence.

MP3 HJ2-3G

Writing Practice

Write the words.

1 ______________ *n* tension	2 ______________ *n* glasses or sunglasses
3 ______________ *v* close both eyes at the same time	4 ______________ *v* fight against
5 ______________ *n* a device to make the air more moist	6 ______________ *v* change

Write the words in each blank.

Summary

There is not enough evidence that ______________ in LED screens is a cause of strained eyes. However, using a computer or ______________ device for a long time is likely to cause eye strain. People can try the 20-20-20 rule or use ______________ tears or a humidifier to ______________ eye strain.

Word Puzzle

Complete the word puzzle.

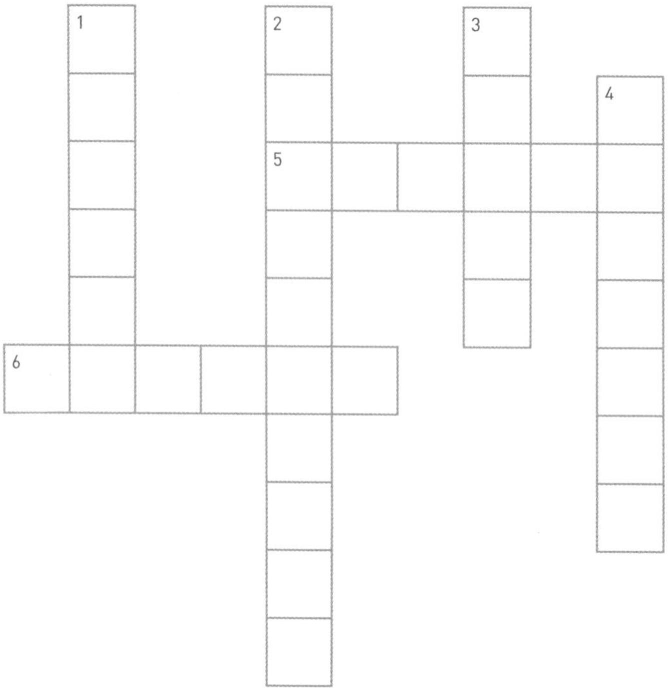

Across

5 change

6 tension

Down

1 fight against

2 a device to make the air more moist

3 close both eyes at the same time

4 glasses or sunglasses

Teacher's Book p.129

UNIT 4

Just One Food

If you were allowed to eat only one type of food, what would you choose? And why?

UNIT 4 Just One Food

While the ideal diet contains diverse foods that provide a full range of vitamins and minerals, in times of crisis humans have had to rely on a limited diet of just one food. For example, when one family of five was shipwrecked for 38 days, they managed to survive primarily off of sea turtle blood. However, if given a survival scenario like a zombie apocalypse, most nutritionists would not choose sea turtle blood. Instead, the lowly potato may be the better option.

The white potato contains large quantities of potassium and iron and has some fiber and protein. It is a food that contains most of the nutrients required by humans, although the amount of each nutrient is very small. Nevertheless, the potato lacks essential elements such as calcium and zinc. A person may be able to survive months eating only potatoes; however, that individual would go blind due to a lack of vitamins. Moreover, the lack of appetite resulting from the boredom of eating just one food would probably lead to starvation first.

Obviously, it is never suggested that people willingly reduce their diet to a single type of food. However, if the zombie apocalypse ever happened and you could only have one food, potatoes might be the best choice.

New Words

diet *n* the kinds of food that someone usually eats	**apocalypse** *n* the end of the world
nutritionist *n* an expert in people's diets	**fiber** *n* a type of material in food that is not digested easily
appetite *n* a desire to eat	**starvation** *n* illness or death from a lack of food

Part A. Picture Description

1.

Malina is a ________.

(A) physicist
(B) humorist
(C) nutritionist
(D) optometrist

2.

Joe has ________ today.

(A) eye strain
(B) no appetite
(C) a lot of work
(D) memory problems

Part B. Sentence Completion

3. ________ the ship we took was large, everyone agreed that it was quite crowded.

(A) While
(B) Despite
(C) As much
(D) Nevertheless

4. You should not limit your diet to ________ type of food.

(A) singly
(B) single
(C) a single
(D) one of single

What would you eat if you could only have one food for the rest of your life?
We asked four Chicago locals this question.

Tracy
Cheeseburgers. On crusty hamburger buns. It wouldn't be as great if I couldn't have fries, too, obviously. But I feel I could live a happy life if all I had was a good supply of cheeseburgers.

Natalia
Noodles. Is there anything better than a tasty mix of noodles and vegetables in black bean sauce? No green onions, though. I'm not a fan.

Jun Young
Mangoes. It's not even that I eat that many mangoes now. But I do like them a lot. If I had to choose, I'd go with that.

Adisa
Pizza. You've got tomatoes, so that's a lot of vitamin C. You've got proteins, carbohydrates, fat, and calcium from the meat, cheese, crust, and oil. With a bunch of green vegetables added on, you've got the perfect food to survive a nuclear war.

5. Which two people prefer something with a bread-like crust?
   (A) Tracy and Natalia
   (B) Natalia and Jun Young
   (C) Jun Young and Adisa
   (D) Adisa and Tracy

6. Which one of these statements would most likely finish one of the Chicago locals' answers?
   (A) "It's my plan to put ketchup on the fries."
   (B) "Just the simple, fruity flavor could sustain me."
   (C) "It's the tomato sauce and noodle combo that I like."
   (D) "Just put green onions on the bean sauce, and you're done."

Part D. General Reading Comprehension

While the ideal diet contains diverse foods that provide a full range of vitamins and minerals, in times of crisis humans have had to rely on a limited diet of just one food. For example, when one family of five was shipwrecked for 38 days, they managed to survive primarily off of sea turtle blood. However, if given a survival scenario like a zombie apocalypse, most nutritionists would not choose sea turtle blood. Instead, the lowly potato may be the better option.

The white potato contains large quantities of potassium and iron and has some fiber and protein. It is a food that contains most of the nutrients required by humans, although the amount of each nutrient is very small. Nevertheless, the potato lacks essential elements such as calcium and zinc. A person may be able to survive months eating only potatoes; however, that individual would go blind due to a lack of vitamins. Moreover, the lack of appetite resulting from the boredom of eating just one food would probably lead to starvation first.

Obviously, it is never suggested that people willingly reduce their diet to a single type of food. However, if the zombie apocalypse ever happened and you could only have one food, potatoes might be the best choice.

7. What is the passage mainly about?
   (A) nutritious ways to prepare food
   (B) the benefits of eating sea turtles
   (C) potatoes as a single food source
   (D) shipwrecks in the middle of the ocean

8. Which is mentioned in the passage?
   (A) red potatoes
   (B) new potatoes
   (C) white potatoes
   (D) moldy potatoes

9. According to the passage, what do potatoes NOT contain?
   (A) iron
   (B) fiber
   (C) calcium
   (D) potassium

10. According to the passage, what could cause starvation?
   (A) liking a food too much
   (B) eating cake every day
   (C) being bored with a food
   (D) drinking water with a meal

Listening Practice

Listen and write.

MP3 HJ2-4

Just One Food

While the ideal 1 __________ contains diverse foods that provide a full range of vitamins and minerals, in times of crisis humans have had to rely on a limited diet of just one food. For example, when one family of five was shipwrecked for 38 days, they managed to survive primarily off of sea turtle blood. However, if given a survival scenario like a zombie 2 __________, most 3 __________ would not choose sea turtle blood. Instead, the lowly potato may be the better option.

The white potato contains large quantities of potassium and iron and has some 4 __________ and protein. It is a food that contains most of the nutrients required by humans, although the amount of each nutrient is very small. Nevertheless, the potato lacks essential elements such as calcium and zinc. A person may be able to survive months eating only potatoes; however, that individual would go blind due to a lack of vitamins. Moreover, the lack of 5 __________ resulting from the boredom of eating just one food would probably lead to 6 __________ first.

Obviously, it is never suggested that people willingly reduce their diet to a single type of food. However, if the zombie apocalypse ever happened and you could only have one food, potatoes might be the best choice.

Word Bank

diets	piber	apetite
apocalypse	fiber	appetite
nutritionists	nutritionist	afocalypse
diet	starvasion	starvation

Listen. Pause. Say each sentence.

MP3 HJ2-4G

Writing Practice

Write the words.

1 ________________ *n* the kinds of food that someone usually eats	2 ________________ *n* the end of the world
3 ________________ *n* an expert in people's diets	4 ________________ *n* a type of material in food that is not digested easily
5 ________________ *n* a desire to eat	6 ________________ *n* illness or death from a lack of food

Write the words in each blank.

Summary

In times of crisis when humans have to rely on a limited ________________ of just one food, potatoes may be the best choice. The ________________ potato contains most of the ________________ required by humans, although the amount of each nutrient is very small and people could get ________________ eating it.

Word Puzzle

Complete the word puzzle.

Across

4 illness or death from a lack of food

6 the end of the world

Down

1 a type of material in food that is not digested easily

2 an expert in people's diets

3 the kinds of food that someone usually eats

5 a desire to eat

AMAZING STORIES

An Allergy to Water

Teacher's Book p.134

Allergy sufferers all over the world have to learn to avoid contact with certain substances. Individuals with a peanut allergy must not eat any foods with traces of peanuts. People with an allergy to wasp stings must avoid those insects. But what happens if someone is afflicted with an allergy to water?

Aquagenic urticaria is the name of the rare condition in which sufferers get rashes as soon as their skin comes in contact with water. Most sufferers are female, and they typically get the condition when they are teenagers. When their skin comes in contact with water, red bumps form on the skin. When the water is removed, the bumps go away 30 minutes to an hour later.

People with aquagenic urticaria can survive because they can usually still drink limited amounts of water. But they must be careful being around water. One sufferer said she can only take five-minute cold showers twice a week. She tries not to sweat or cry, and she must not be out in the rain.

The allergy's cause is a mystery to medical scientists. It is thought that it is probably not water itself but rather something inside the water that is causing the allergy. Otherwise, there could be something in the water that is reacting with something in the allergy sufferer's skin. Still, why this condition occurs and how it can be stopped are mysteries in the field of health.

CHAPTER 2

Environment

Teacher's Book
p.135

UNIT 5

Climate Change

List three things that you know about climate change.

Climate Change

As humankind contributes more heat-trapping gases to the earth's atmosphere, climate change continues to disrupt the planet's natural systems. While many effects are already underway, scientists predict that within the next century other major impacts will occur.

The documented current impacts of climate change are numerous. They include melting Arctic sea ice as well as mountain glaciers. As a result of the melting ice, oceans are rising and certain wildlife species, such as sea turtles, are disappearing. At the same time, some invasive species are increasing, including Lyme disease-carrying ticks. Average rain and snowfall have risen across the entire planet, and at the same time some regions have seen more droughts, leading to water shortages.

Within the next decades other impacts are predicted to occur. Rising ocean temperatures will likely cause many worsening problems. Among these are stronger hurricanes, more intense heatwaves, less freshwater, and the spread of certain diseases such as malaria due to increased numbers of mosquitoes.

Climate change is real, and its many effects are drastic. Without immediate and aggressive action from governments around the world, it is unlikely that the intensification of these effects will be stopped or even slowed.

New Words

underway *adj* happening	documented *adj* recorded
invasive species *n* a non-native species taking over an ecosystem	tick *n* a small insect that sucks blood
drought *n* a long period with no rain	drastic *adj* extreme

10 minutes

Part A. Picture Description

1.

This area is experiencing a ________.

(A) flood
(B) drought
(C) hurricane
(D) landslide

2.

There has been a ________ fall in the stock market.

(A) slight
(B) drastic
(C) negligible
(D) moderate

Part B. Sentence Completion

3. Many regions have been ________ impacted by the weather.

(A) heavy
(B) heavily
(C) a heavy
(D) such heavily

4. It is highly unlikely ________ these effects will lessen.

(A) for
(B) that
(C) feel
(D) to see

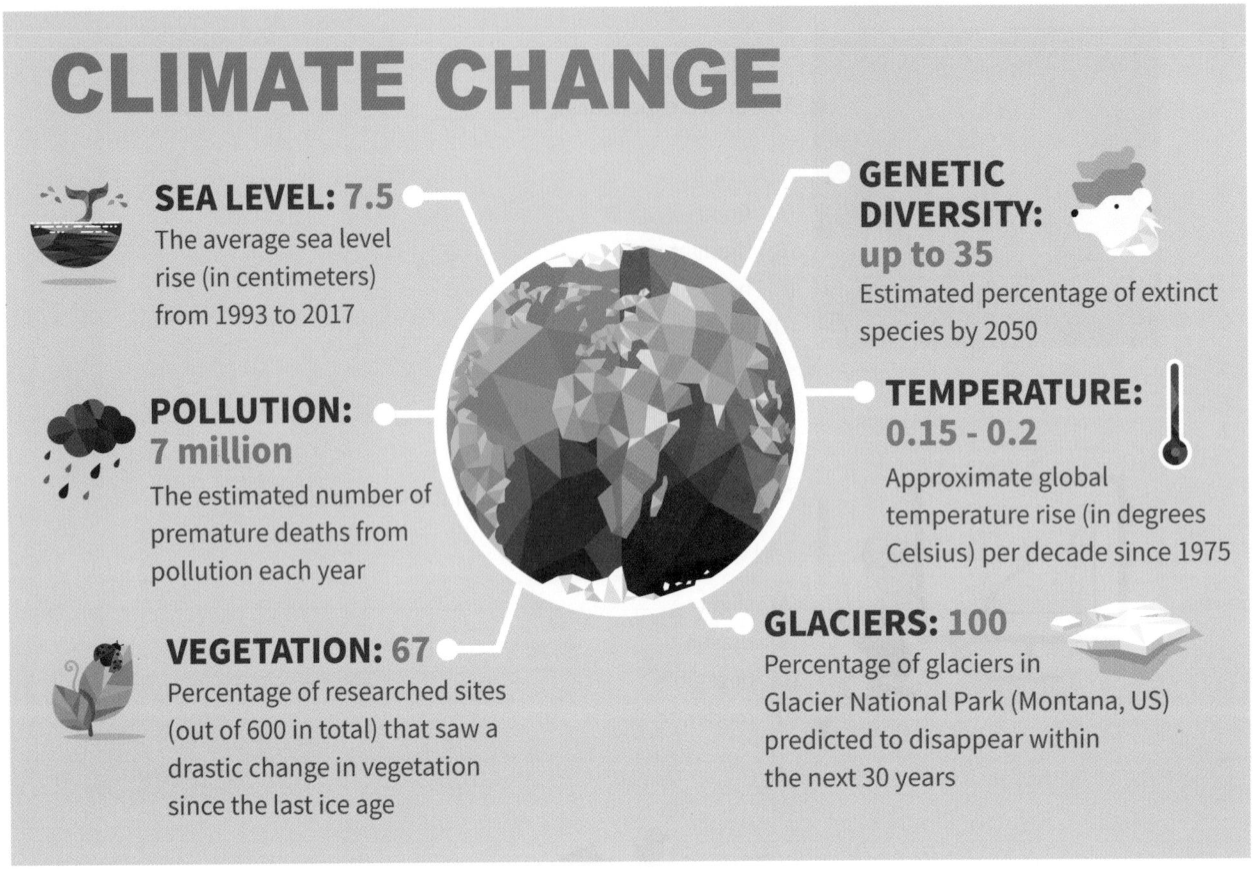

5. According to the infographic, what does 0.15 refer to?

(A) percentage rate of increase in sea levels globally
(B) people (in billions) who will die prematurely from micro-dust
(C) degrees that global temperature has risen since the seventies
(D) number of plants (in millions) that will disappear within thirty years

6. What does the infographic state regarding glaciers?

(A) One hundred known glaciers in Antarctica are melting.
(B) Most of the glaciers in a national park have shrunk by 30%
(C) There are only 100 polar bears left in Glacier National Park.
(D) All of the ones in a US park could be gone in three decades.

Part D. General Reading Comprehension

As humankind contributes more heat-trapping gases to the earth's atmosphere, climate change continues to disrupt the planet's natural systems. While many effects are already underway, scientists predict that within the next century other major impacts will occur.

The documented current impacts of climate change are numerous. They include melting Arctic sea ice as well as mountain glaciers. As a result of the melting ice, oceans are rising and certain wildlife species, such as sea turtles, are disappearing. At the same time, some invasive species are increasing, including Lyme disease-carrying ticks. Average rain and snowfall have risen across the entire planet, and at the same time some regions have seen more droughts, leading to water shortages.

Within the next decades other impacts are predicted to occur. Rising ocean temperatures will likely cause many worsening problems. Among these are stronger hurricanes, more intense heatwaves, less freshwater, and the spread of certain diseases such as malaria due to increased numbers of mosquitoes.

Climate change is real, and its many effects are drastic. Without immediate and aggressive action from governments around the world, it is unlikely that the intensification of these effects will be stopped or even slowed.

7. What would be the best title for the passage?
(A) Climate Change Effects
(B) The Science of Weather
(C) Sea Levels and Climate Change
(D) Individuals and the Environment

8. What ocean creatures are mentioned in the passage?
(A) coral
(B) turtles
(C) whales
(D) jellyfish

9. According to the passage, what may increase?
(A) cases of malaria
(B) human population
(C) polar bear attacks
(D) the number of farms

10. Which would best describe the tone of the passage?
(A) romantic
(B) optimistic
(C) apologetic
(D) pessimistic

Listening Practice

Listen and write.

MP3 HJ2-5

Climate Change

As humankind contributes more heat-trapping gases to the earth's atmosphere, climate change continues to disrupt the planet's natural systems. While many effects are already 1 ________, scientists predict that within the next century other major impacts will occur.

The 2 ________ current impacts of climate change are numerous. They include melting Arctic sea ice as well as mountain glaciers. As a result of the melting ice, oceans are rising and certain wildlife species, such as sea turtles, are disappearing. At the same time, some 3 ________ species are increasing, including Lyme disease-carrying 4 ________. Average rain and snowfall have risen across the entire planet, and at the same time some regions have seen more 5 ________, leading to water shortages.

Within the next decades other impacts are predicted to occur. Rising ocean temperatures will likely cause many worsening problems. Among these are stronger hurricanes, more intense heatwaves, less freshwater, and the spread of certain diseases such as malaria due to increased numbers of mosquitoes.

Climate change is real, and its many effects are 6 ________. Without immediate and aggressive action from governments around the world, it is unlikely that the intensification of these effects will be stopped or even slowed.

Word Bank

underweigh	invasive	documented
document	ticks	drestic
underway	droughts	tix
drastic	inbasive	drowts

Listen. Pause. Say each sentence.

MP3 HJ2-5G

Writing Practice

Write the words.

1 ______________ *adj* happening	2 ______________ *adj* recorded
3 ______________ *n* a non-native species taking over an ecosystem	4 ______________ *n* a small insect that sucks blood
5 ______________ *n* a long period with no rain	6 ______________ *adj* extreme

Write the words in each blank.

Summary

While many effects from climate change are ______________, it is predicted that within the next century other major impacts will ______________. If governments around the world do not ______________ immediate action, the intensification of these ______________ is unlikely to be stopped or even slowed.

Word Puzzle

Complete the word puzzle.

Across

1 a small insect that sucks blood

3 extreme

4 happening

5 recorded

Down

2 a non-native species taking over an ecosystem

5 a long period with no rain

Teacher's Book
p.140

UNIT 6

Drone-based Delivery

Have you ever seen someone using a drone?
What were they using it for? Have you tried using a drone?

UNIT 6 Drone-based Delivery

Increased capabilities by drones have prompted online retailers to explore drone-based delivery as an alternative to delivery by trucks. Proponents of this new type of service claim that not only can it help clear traffic from streets, but that it could also save energy.

However, some researchers argue that whether or not an electric-powered drone saves energy is not so obvious. It depends on what kind of fuel the truck uses, how large the drone is, and what needs to be delivered. Where the energy is produced matters as some regions have more environmentally friendly ways of making electricity. The weight of the package matters, too. A drone requires a lot of energy to be able to take off from the ground carrying a heavy item. Furthermore, trucks do not necessarily need to run on fossil fuels. They could be electric-powered vehicles, and the electricity could be generated from low CO_2-creating sources, such as wind or solar power.

One group of environmental scientists claims that a system might be more energy-efficient if heavier packages are delivered by electric-powered vehicles and single light packages are delivered by electric-powered drones. It will be interesting to find out how drone-based delivery can be adjusted for maximum energy efficiency in the future.

New Words

prompt *v* cause	**retailer** *n* a business that sells goods in smaller quantities (not a wholesaler)
proponent *n* a supporter	**claim** *v* argue
fossil fuel *n* coal or gas	**adjust** *v* modify

Part A. Picture Description

1.

They are aiming to get ________.

(A) fossil fuels
(B) wind farms
(C) tidal energy
(D) solar power

2.

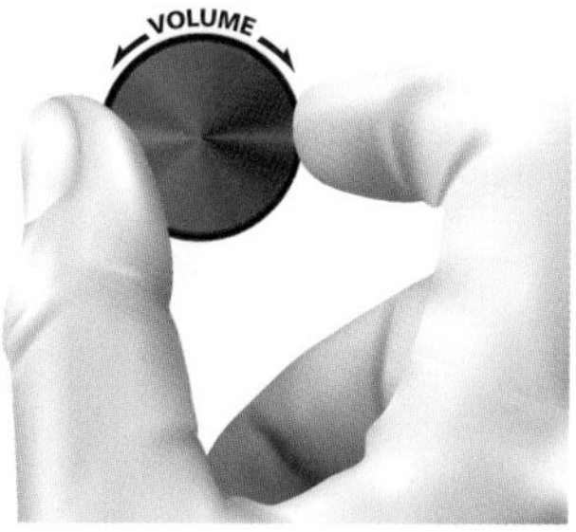

He is ________ the volume.

(A) turning
(B) moving
(C) adjusting
(D) fashioning

Part B. Sentence Completion

3. Do I like dogs? It really depends ________ the dog.

(A) at
(B) in
(C) on
(D) for

4. Proponents of the new law ________ that it will help delivery drivers.

(A) claim
(B) claims
(C) are claim
(D) has claimed

- Light as a feather
- State-of-the-art technology
- Can take precision photographic shots of the desired environment
- Can be used to monitor: deforestation, melting glaciers, disappearing species.

Researchers: <u>**Click here**</u> for more information about how this drone can help you to help the environment!

5. Which of the following would best go in the blank?

   (A) Fun Drone for Kids
   (B) Lightweight Eco-Drone
   (C) Classroom Monitor Drone
   (D) Photography for Festivals

6. Which of the following is NOT mentioned?

   (A) uses of the drone
   (B) how the drone charges
   (C) how to get further details
   (D) the modernity of the technology

Part D. General Reading Comprehension

Increased capabilities by drones have prompted online retailers to explore drone-based delivery as an alternative to delivery by trucks. Proponents of this new type of service claim that not only can it help clear traffic from streets, but that it could also save energy.

However, some researchers argue that whether or not an electric-powered drone saves energy is not so obvious. It depends on what kind of fuel the truck uses, how large the drone is, and what needs to be delivered. Where the energy is produced matters as some regions have more environmentally friendly ways of making electricity. The weight of the package matters, too. A drone requires a lot of energy to be able to take off from the ground carrying a heavy item. Furthermore, trucks do not necessarily need to run on fossil fuels. They could be electric-powered vehicles, and the electricity could be generated from low CO_2-creating sources, such as wind or solar power.

One group of environmental scientists claims that a system might be more energy-efficient if heavier packages are delivered by electric-powered vehicles and single light packages are delivered by electric-powered drones. It will be interesting to find out how drone-based delivery can be adjusted for maximum energy efficiency in the future.

7. What is the main topic of the passage?
   (A) drones for environment surveillance
   (B) saving money through online shopping
   (C) drone-based versus truck-based delivery
   (D) self-driving vehicles versus human-driven ones

8. Which of the following is NOT mentioned?
   (A) truck fuel
   (B) drone size
   (C) vehicle color
   (D) package weight

9. According to the passage, why does it matter where the energy is produced?
   (A) Certain cities sell their electricity for a profit.
   (B) Many countries have too little sunshine for solar power.
   (C) A few regions have a ban on using electricity for drones.
   (D) Some places have more environmentally friendly energy production.

10. According to the passage, which delivery method is recommended by a group of environmental scientists for a small, individual package?
   (A) diesel truck
   (B) electric truck
   (C) electric drone
   (D) gas-powered drone

Listening Practice

Listen and write.

MP3 HJ2-6

Drone-based Delivery

Increased capabilities by drones have [1] ______ online [2] ______ to explore drone-based delivery as an alternative to delivery by trucks. [3] ______ of this new type of service [4] ______ that not only can it help clear traffic from streets, but that it could also save energy.

However, some researchers argue that whether or not an electric-powered drone saves energy is not so obvious. It depends on what kind of fuel the truck uses, how large the drone is, and what needs to be delivered. Where the energy is produced matters as some regions have more environmentally friendly ways of making electricity. The weight of the package matters, too. A drone requires a lot of energy to be able to take off from the ground carrying a heavy item. Furthermore, trucks do not necessarily need to run on fossil [5] ______. They could be electric-powered vehicles, and the electricity could be generated from low CO_2-creating sources, such as wind or solar power.

One group of environmental scientists claims that a system might be more energy-efficient if heavier packages are delivered by electric-powered vehicles and single light packages are delivered by electric-powered drones. It will be interesting to find out how drone-based delivery can be [6] ______ for maximum energy efficiency in the future.

Word Bank

proponents	ajusted	fyools
retalers	fuels	adjusted
clame	Proponents	prompted
retailers	prompt	claim

Listen. Pause. Say each sentence.

MP3 HJ2-6G

Writing Practice

Write the words.

1 ________________ *v* cause	2 ________________ *n* a business that sells goods in smaller quantities (not a wholesaler)
3 ________________ *n* a supporter	4 ________________ *v* argue
5 ________________ *n* coal or gas	6 ________________ *v* modify

Write the words in each blank.

Summary

As capabilities by drones have increased, online retailers have ________________ drone-based ________________ as an ________________ to delivery by trucks. While supporters of drone-based delivery say it will save energy, some researchers argue that whether or not an electric-powered drone ________________ energy is not so obvious for many reasons.

Word Puzzle

Complete the word puzzle.

Across

4 coal or gas

5 cause

Down

1 a business that sells goods in smaller quantities (not a wholesaler)

2 modify

3 argue

5 a supporter

Teacher's Book
p.145

UNIT 7

The Nene

Which birds are protected in your region?

UNIT 7 The Nene

The nene, also known as the Hawaiian goose, is a bird that can only be found on the islands of Hawaii. Scientists believe that Canada geese came to Hawaii when the islands first formed 500,000 years ago. They slowly evolved into this new species. This new type of goose made a soft sound like "nay, nay," and so the Hawaiians called the bird "nene."

The population of nene has declined ever since the Western explorers first visited the islands in 1778. Estimates state there may have been as many as 25,000 nene at the time. However, many of the explorers hunted them, and new enemies like cats and pigs reduced the nene's numbers. By the early 1950s, there were only about thirty of the birds remaining. They were considered endangered and about to disappear forever.

Thankfully, zoologists worked very hard to save them. It took many years and a lot of effort, but by 2018 there were nearly 3,000 nene living on the Hawaiian islands, both in zoos and in nature. Some scientists and government officials even suggest that the nene can be taken off the list of endangered animals because of the successful efforts to save them.

New Words

goose n a bird like a large duck	evolve v adapt over time
decline v go down	estimate n a rough calculation
endangered adj in danger of going extinct	suggest v propose

Part A. Picture Description

1.

These Canada ________ will fly south in the winter.

(A) geese
(B) herons
(C) canaries
(D) ducklings

2.

The value has ________.

(A) jumped
(B) declined
(C) skyrocketed
(D) accumulated

Part B. Sentence Completion

3. New York, ________ the Big Apple, has a fascinating history.

(A) also known as
(B) is also known
(C) which also knows as
(D) which as also known

4. By the sixties there were only a few of those sharks left. ________ the numbers been so low.

(A) Had never before
(B) Never had before
(C) We had before never
(D) There never before had

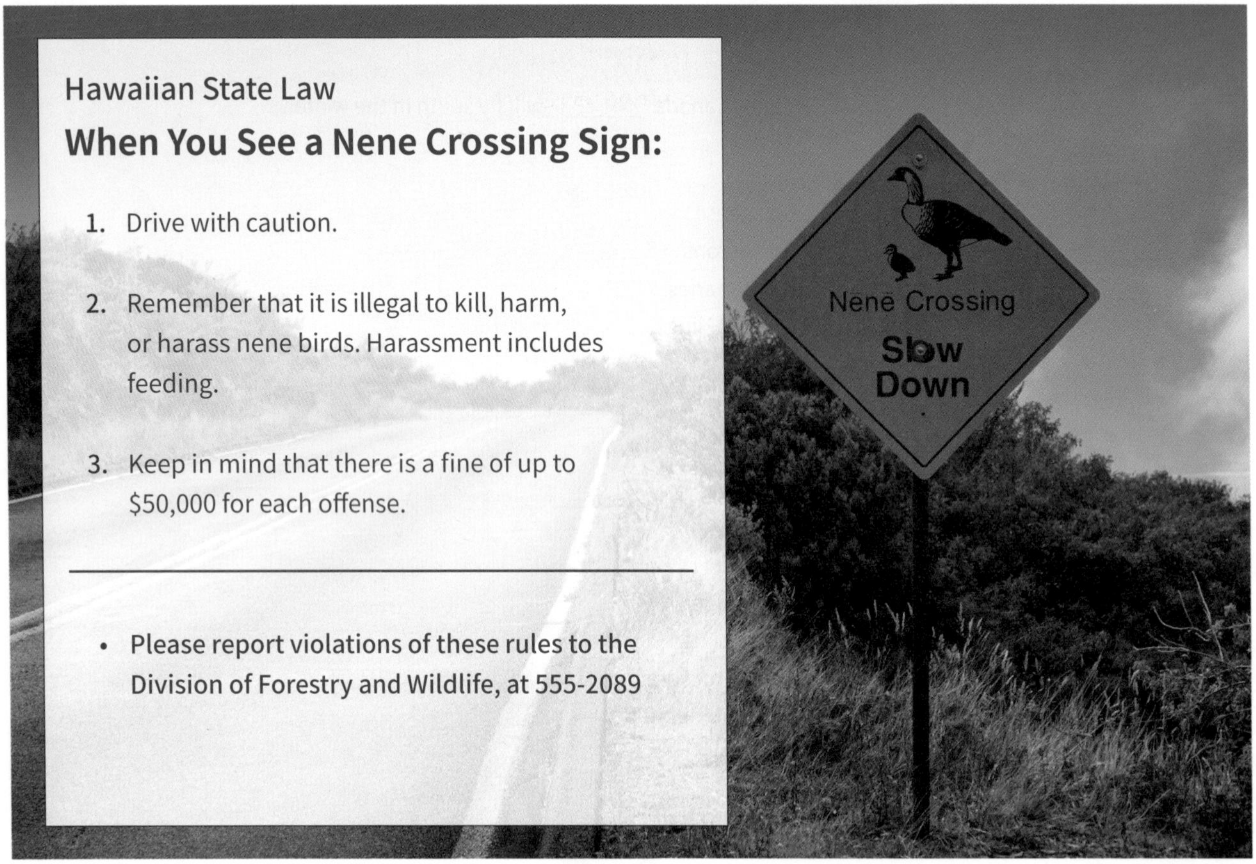

Hawaiian State Law

When You See a Nene Crossing Sign:

1. Drive with caution.
2. Remember that it is illegal to kill, harm, or harass nene birds. Harassment includes feeding.
3. Keep in mind that there is a fine of up to $50,000 for each offense.

- **Please report violations of these rules to the Division of Forestry and Wildlife, at 555-2089**

5. Where would the announcement most likely NOT be posted?

   (A) on a road sign
   (B) on a website for drivers
   (C) in a Hawaii tourist guide
   (D) in a Guam police station

6. According to the notice, what is true?

   (A) It is against the law to feed nene birds.
   (B) Driving in areas with nene birds is illegal.
   (C) Rule-breakers should be arrested immediately.
   (D) Tourists who harm a nene bird will be deported.

Part D. General Reading Comprehension

The nene, also known as the Hawaiian goose, is a bird that can only be found on the islands of Hawaii. Scientists believe that Canada geese came to Hawaii when the islands first formed 500,000 years ago. They slowly evolved into this new species. This new type of goose made a soft sound like "nay, nay," and so the Hawaiians called the bird "nene."

The population of nene has declined ever since the Western explorers first visited the islands in 1778. Estimates state there may have been as many as 25,000 nene at the time. However, many of the explorers hunted them, and new enemies like cats and pigs reduced the nene's numbers. By the early 1950s, there were only about thirty of the birds remaining. They were considered endangered and about to disappear forever.

Thankfully, zoologists worked very hard to save them. It took many years and a lot of effort, but by 2018 there were nearly 3,000 nene living on the Hawaiian islands, both in zoos and in nature. Some scientists and government officials even suggest that the nene can be taken off the list of endangered animals because of the successful efforts to save them.

7. Which would be the best title for the passage?

(A) Where Do Nene Live?
(B) What Killed off the Nene?
(C) How the Nene Got Its Name
(D) Hope for an Endangered Bird

8. Where do nene live?

(A) Fiji
(B) Alaska
(C) Canada
(D) Hawaii

9. When did the nene population start to go down?

(A) in the 1770s
(B) in the 1800s
(C) in the 1950s
(D) in the 2010s

10. Which of the following groups did NOT contribute to the nene's decline?

(A) pigs
(B) cats
(C) explorers
(D) zoologists

Listening Practice

Listen and write.

MP3 HJ2-7

The Nene

The nene, also known as the Hawaiian [1] ________, is a bird that can only be found on the islands of Hawaii. Scientists believe that Canada geese came to Hawaii when the islands first formed 500,000 years ago. They slowly [2] ________ into this new species. This new type of goose made a soft sound like "nay, nay," and so the Hawaiians called the bird "nene." The population of nene has [3] ________ ever since the Western explorers first visited the islands in 1778. [4] ________ state there may have been as many as 25,000 nene at the time. However, many of the explorers hunted them, and new enemies like cats and pigs reduced the nene's numbers. By the early 1950s, there were only about thirty of the birds remaining. They were considered [5] ________ and about to disappear forever. Thankfully, zoologists worked very hard to save them. It took many years and a lot of effort, but by 2018 there were nearly 3,000 nene living on the Hawaiian islands, both in zoos and in nature. Some scientists and government officials even [6] ________ that the nene can be taken off the list of endangered animals because of the successful efforts to save them.

Word Bank

evolved	endangered	geese
sugest	Estimates	declined
goose	indangered	declind
ebulbed	suggest	estimates

Listen. Pause. Say each sentence.

MP3 HJ2-7G

Writing Practice

Write the words.

1 ________________ *n* a bird like a large duck	2 ________________ *v* adapt over time
3 ________________ *v* go down	4 ________________ *n* a rough calculation
5 ________________ *adj* in danger of going extinct	6 ________________ *v* propose

Write the words in each blank.

Summary

In the early 1950s, the population of nene became so small that the bird was considered ________________ and about to disappear. Thankfully, ________________ worked very hard to ________________ them. Because of these successful efforts, some propose that the nene can now be ________________ off the endangered animal list.

Word Puzzle

Complete the word puzzle.

Across

5 in danger of going extinct

6 adapt over time

Down

1 a rough calculation

2 a bird like a large duck

3 propose

4 go down

Teacher's Book p.151

UNIT 8

The Amazon

Think! Does the Amazon River flow west to east or east to west?

UNIT 8 The Amazon

Looking at a map today, one can see that the Amazon flows from west to east. The world's second longest river starts in the Andes Mountains of Peru and takes a long, winding path across South America until it reaches the Atlantic Ocean in the East. The Amazon River transports more water to the ocean than any other river. It would seem that such a large body of water would not see drastic changes in its history, but researchers have found that not to be true.

When the continents of South America and Africa were still connected millions of years ago, the Amazon and the Congo were one river system that flowed from east to west. Then as South America broke away from Africa, the Amazon's flow began to change. First, a small mountain range grew up halfway down the river, causing water to flow from the center of the continent to the oceans on both sides. Eventually, however, the Andes Mountains formed on the western side of South America. These mountains became extremely tall, causing all of the water of the Amazon River to flow away from them in the direction everyone knows today.

New Words

winding *adj* curvy	**body of water** *n* a collection of water
continent *n* a continuous mass of land	**break away** *v* separate
flow *v* move (for liquids)	**eventually** *adv* in the end

Part A. Picture Description

1.

The long ________ road goes through the hills.

(A) gravel
(B) straight
(C) winding
(D) cobblestoned

2.

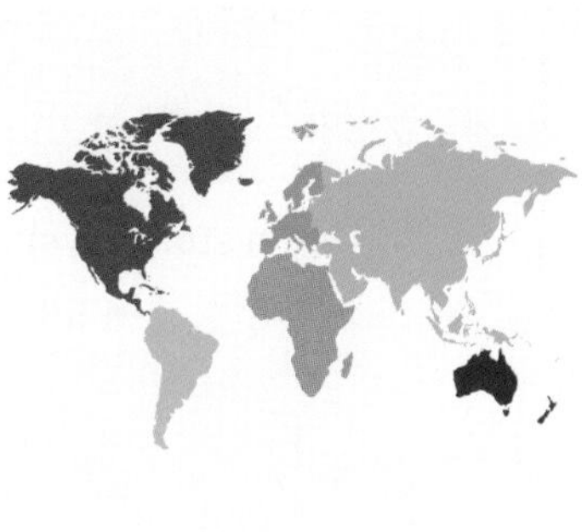

On this map, each ________ is a different color.

(A) city
(B) country
(C) college
(D) continent

Part B. Sentence Completion

3. Jenna did more for our charity last year than ________ other volunteer.

(A) all
(B) any
(C) each
(D) either

4. At first I didn't want to go on the trip. Eventually, ________, I decided to go and ended up having a wonderful time.

(A) despite
(B) whereas
(C) however
(D) although

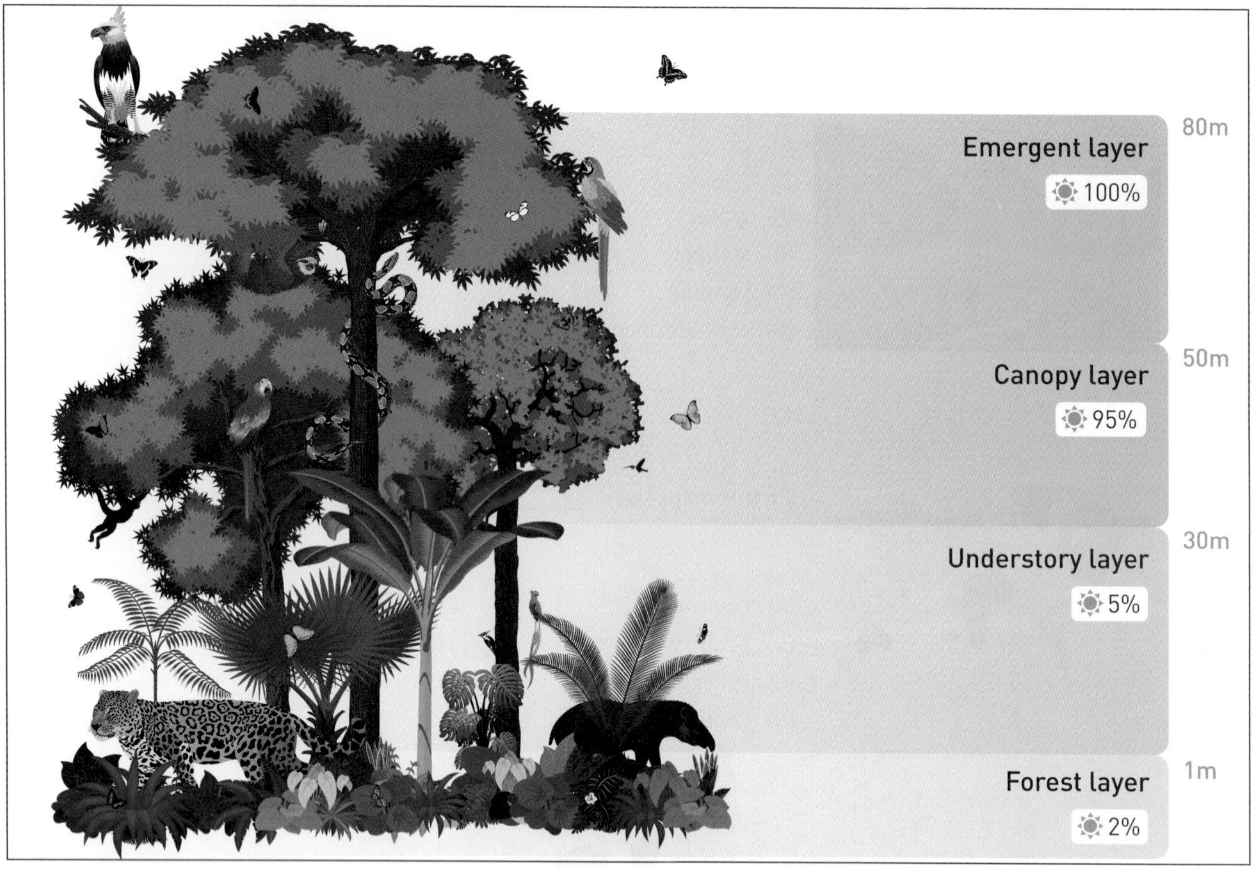

5. According to the picture, where does the emergent layer begin?
   (A) below the 30 m level
   (B) at 30 m from the canopy
   (C) at 50 m from the ground
   (D) at 80 m from the understory

6. According to the picture, which of the following is true about sunshine?
   (A) The forest floor gets less than 1 percent.
   (B) The emergent layer gets the least amount of all the layers.
   (C) The understory gets 3 percentage points more than the forest floor.
   (D) The canopy gets up to 50 percentage points more than the understory.

Part D. General Reading Comprehension

Looking at a map today, one can see that the Amazon flows from west to east. The world's second longest river starts in the Andes Mountains of Peru and takes a long, winding path across South America until it reaches the Atlantic Ocean in the East. The Amazon River transports more water to the ocean than any other river. It would seem that such a large body of water would not see drastic changes in its history, but researchers have found that not to be true.

When the continents of South America and Africa were still connected millions of years ago, the Amazon and the Congo were one river system that flowed from east to west. Then as South America broke away from Africa, the Amazon's flow began to change. First, a small mountain range grew up halfway down the river, causing water to flow from the center of the continent to the oceans on both sides. Eventually, however, the Andes Mountains formed on the western side of South America. These mountains became extremely tall, causing all of the water of the Amazon River to flow away from them in the direction everyone knows today.

7. What is the main idea of the passage?
   (A) South America used to be smaller.
   (B) South America and Africa were once connected.
   (C) The water of the Amazon River is turning a new color.
   (D) The flow of the Amazon River changed direction over time.

8. What fact about the Amazon is NOT mentioned?
   (A) It reaches the Atlantic Ocean.
   (B) It has no bridges built across it.
   (C) It starts in the Andes Mountains.
   (D) It is the world's second longest river.

9. According to the passage, what caused the water to flow to both oceans?
   (A) storms
   (B) tsunamis
   (C) mountains
   (D) rainforests

10. According to the passage, where did a mountain range rise?
   (A) in the center of Central America
   (B) at the start of the Amazon River
   (C) in the middle of the Amazon River
   (D) at the southernmost tip of South America

Listening Practice

Listen and write.

MP3 HJ2-8

The Amazon

Looking at a map today, one can see that the Amazon flows from west to east. The world's second longest river starts in the Andes Mountains of Peru and takes a long, 1 __________ path across South America until it reaches the Atlantic Ocean in the East. The Amazon River transports more water to the ocean than any other river. It would seem that such a large 2 __________ would not see drastic changes in its history, but researchers have found that not to be true.

When the 3 __________ of South America and Africa were still connected millions of years ago, the Amazon and the Congo were one river system that flowed from east to west. Then as South America 4 __________ from Africa, the Amazon's flow began to change. First, a small mountain range grew up halfway down the river, causing water to flow from the center of the continent to the oceans on both sides. 5 __________, however, the Andes Mountains formed on the western side of South America. These mountains became extremely tall, causing all of the water of the Amazon River to 6 __________ away from them in the direction everyone knows today.

Word Bank

continants	winding	body of water
flow	flo	Eventualy
Eventually	broke away	broke of way
continents	body evwater	windy

Listen. Pause. Say each sentence.

MP3 HJ2-8G

Writing Practice

Write the words.

1 ________ *adj* curvy	2 ________ *n* a collection of water
3 ________ *n* a continuous mass of land	4 ________ *v* separate
5 ________ *v* move (for liquids)	6 ________ *adv* in the end

Write the words in each blank.

Summary

It is found that the water of the Amazon River have changed ________ in its history. The ________ of the Amazon River changed over time. Eventually when the Andes Mountains ________, all of the water of the Amazon River started to flow away from them, in the ________ everyone knows now.

Word Puzzle

Complete the word puzzle.

Across

1 a collection of water

4 curvy

5 move (for liquids)

Down

1 separate

2 in the end

3 a continuous mass of land

Vaan Irai Kal: The Sky God's Stone

Teacher's Book p.156

In the town of Mahabalipuram, Tamil Nadu, India, there is a strange sight. A huge boulder of rock – 6 meters high, 5 meters wide, and weighing 250 tons – appears to have rolled down a steep hill. However, just at the edge of a hill, it seems to have stopped. It now sits there, suspended over the hill. And no matter how hard they try, people attempting to move the huge stone cannot get the boulder to budge. This is the mystery of the Vaan Irai Kal (Sky God's Stone).

Adding a sense of playfulness to the story of the Vaan Irai Kal is its nickname: "Krishna's Butterball." According to Hindu myths, lord Krishna used to enjoy butter when he was just a baby. The Vaan Irai Kal is thus like a ball of butter that Krishna dropped. It is said that either a tour guide in Mahabalipuram or India's prime minister gave the stone the name "Krishna's Butterball," and that the name proved popular.

The giant boulder is an impressive environmental mystery. It is thought that its odd position may have been due to either a glacier that moved or due to abrasion from the wind over a long time. It is also thought that an important reason for the boulder's seemingly impossible balancing act is really just the position of its center of gravity. An alternative theory is that the rock was carved by humans a long time ago.

Whatever the reason for its existence, Krishna's Butterball is now a major tourist attraction and an environmental wonder in the area.

CHAPTER 3

Science

Teacher's Book
p.157

UNIT 9

Memory

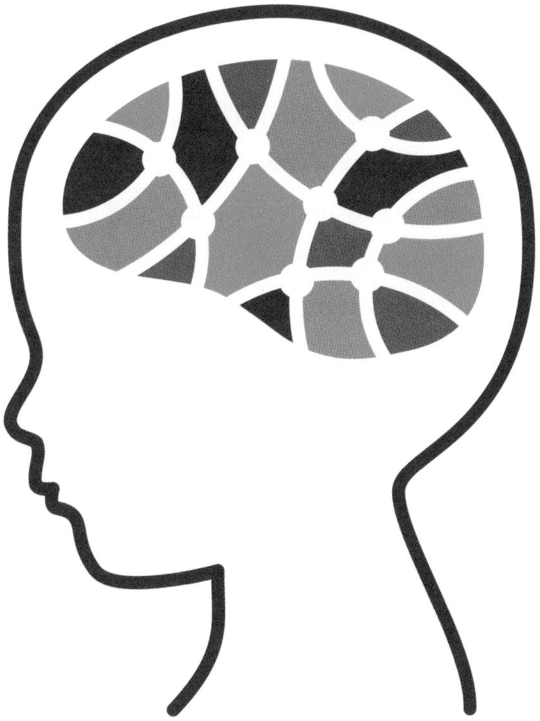

Do you have a good memory?
Describe a really happy memory in your life.

UNIT 9 Memory

Thanks to modern technology, scientists have learned more about how the human brain works. Now, researchers have new explanations of how memories are created.

Memory can be broadly divided into short-term and long-term types. Short-term memory is our ability to remember things just fifteen to thirty seconds after they happen. With long-term memory, neurons in the brain make actual new physical connections with one another. These connections are called synapses. Long-term memory can be further divided into implicit and explicit memory. Our implicit memories are habits, like riding a bike, whereas explicit memories relate to moments or information we have to actively work on remembering.

When we learn to do something, we start with explicit memory, and this may become part of our implicit memory. To form an explicit memory, the hippocampus area of the brain creates new synapses that can encode a piece of information. The hippocampus selects what will become a long-term memory. Information with a lot of emotions connected to it is more likely to be chosen for encoding. New memories seem to stay in the hippocampus for a short time. Then, the clump of neurons that forms the memory moves further into the brain. These long-term memories can now be accessed, and very importantly, strengthened by being activated.

New Words

broadly *adv* largely	neuron *n* a nerve cell
implicit *adj* passive, without being expressed	explicit *adj* actively expressed
clump *n* a solid mass of something	activate *v* trigger

10 minutes

Part A. Picture Description

1.

Ana's favorite toy was just a ________ of string with eyes.

(A) bag
(B) bottle
(C) clump
(D) container

2.

He is about to ________ a machine.

(A) create
(B) invent
(C) activate
(D) dissemble

Part B. Sentence Completion

3. ________ online maps, it is now easy to find any location on Earth.

(A) Thanks
(B) Thanks to
(C) Thanks be
(D) Thanks go to

4. Information with a lot of emotions connected to it ________ more likely to be remembered.

(A) is
(B) are
(C) would
(D) should

Fun with Neuroscience!
90,459 views

Video posted by:
The Pewland University of Technology

Published on Aug 16, 2017

Marzie
The cartoons in the video were a bit silly, but this actually helped me study for my brain science quiz!

Karl
This was actually pretty interesting.

Jason
Awesome video! So cool! Just kidding—this was probably the dumbest video ever.

> **Seth**
> What's wrong? Got problems with your hippocampus?
>
> **Jason**
> No, YOU do. Your hippocampus is totally broken.
>
> **Seth**
> Not responding. Instead I'll watch this video again and improve my brain...

Chau
I honestly think this video helped me to form new synapses. Short-term to long-term memories are being formed, people!

> **Marzie**
> Ha ha ha! YESSSSS!

5. Who did NOT enjoy the video?

(A) Marzie
(B) Karl
(C) Jason
(D) Seth

6. According to the comments, which of the following is true?

(A) Karl found the video boring but useful.
(B) Seth was planning to rewatch the video.
(C) Chau forgot most of what he learned from the video.
(D) Marzie thought the video's artwork was the best part.

Part D. General Reading Comprehension

Thanks to modern technology, scientists have learned more about how the human brain works. Now, researchers have new explanations of how memories are created.

Memory can be broadly divided into short-term and long-term types. Short-term memory is our ability to remember things just fifteen to thirty seconds after they happen. With long-term memory, neurons in the brain make actual new physical connections with one another. These connections are called synapses. Long-term memory can be further divided into implicit and explicit memory. Our implicit memories are habits, like riding a bike, whereas explicit memories relate to moments or information we have to actively work on remembering.

When we learn to do something, we start with explicit memory, and this may become part of our implicit memory. To form an explicit memory, the hippocampus area of the brain creates new synapses that can encode a piece of information. The hippocampus selects what will become a long-term memory. Information with a lot of emotions connected to it is more likely to be chosen for encoding. New memories seem to stay in the hippocampus for a short time. Then, the clump of neurons that forms the memory moves further into the brain. These long-term memories can now be accessed, and very importantly, strengthened by being activated.

7. What would be the best title for the passage?
   (A) Reasons Why We Forget
   (B) How Memories Are Created
   (C) Where Memories Are Stored
   (D) All About Short-Term Memory

8. According to the passage, what is short-term memory?
   (A) 7-day memory
   (B) overnight memory
   (C) memory from noon to midnight
   (D) memory of events 15-30 second prior

9. According to the passage, what kind of memory is most likely involved when an experienced cyclist rides a bike?
   (A) implicit memory
   (B) explicit memory
   (C) vacuum memory
   (D) neurotic memory

10. Which kind of memory is the hippocampus more likely to select to keep?
   (A) a visual memory
   (B) an emotional memory
   (C) one from a realistic dream
   (D) one from a person's childhood

Listening Practice

Listen and write.

MP3 HJ2-9

Memory

Thanks to modern technology, scientists have learned more about how the human brain works. Now, researchers have new explanations of how memories are created.

Memory can be 1 __________ divided into short-term and long-term types. Short-term memory is our ability to remember things just fifteen to thirty seconds after they happen. With long-term memory, 2 __________ in the brain make actual new physical connections with one another. These connections are called synapses. Long-term memory can be further divided into 3 __________ and 4 __________ memory. Our implicit memories are habits, like riding a bike, whereas explicit memories relate to moments or information we have to actively work on remembering.

When we learn to do something, we start with explicit memory, and this may become part of our implicit memory. To form an explicit memory, the hippocampus area of the brain creates new synapses that can encode a piece of information. The hippocampus selects what will become a long-term memory. Information with a lot of emotions connected to it is more likely to be chosen for encoding. New memories seem to stay in the hippocampus for a short time. Then, the 5 __________ of neurons that forms the memory moves further into the brain. These long-term memories can now be accessed, and very importantly, strengthened by being 6 __________.

Word Bank

brodly	impliccit	expliccit
activated	broadly	explicit
clamp	activate	implicit
clump	neurons	neurrons

Listen. Pause. Say each sentence.

MP3 HJ2-9G

Writing Practice

Write the words.

1 ______________ *adv* largely	2 ______________ *n* a nerve cell
3 ______________ *adj* passive, without being expressed	4 ______________ *adj* actively expressed
5 ______________ *n* a solid mass of something	6 ______________ *v* trigger

Write the words in each blank.

Summary

Memory can be divided into short-term and ______________ types. Our brain goes through many processes to ______________ our long-term memories. These memories can then be ______________ and strengthened by being ______________.

Word Puzzle

Complete the word puzzle.

Across

2 largely

4 passive, without being expressed

5 a solid mass of something

6 a nerve cell

Down

1 actively expressed

3 trigger

Teacher's Book
p.162

UNIT 10

Phases of the Moon

Think about a time when the moon looked special.
When was it? Where were you?

UNIT 10 Phases of the Moon

Every 29.53 days (a lunar month), the moon goes through a cycle of darkness, light, and different shapes to the human eye. We call this the waxing (getting bigger) and waning (getting smaller) of the moon.

In western cultures, waxing and waning comprises eight phases. In the first phase, the moon appears completely dark to those of us on Earth as the sun and moon are aligned. This is called the New Moon. The next phase is the Waxing Crescent Moon, where we can start to see a little sliver of the moon. The sliver keeps growing and reaches the First Quarter Moon, the phase in which the moon has now completed a fourth of its orbit around the earth. At the First Quarter, the moon looks like a perfect half-circle from Earth. The Waxing Gibbous Moon phase comes next. "Gibbous" refers to the specific shape of the moon here – bigger than a semi-circle, but not yet a full circle. Finally, the moon gets to the Full Moon, where the moon looks like a full circle. The other phases, called Waning Gibbous Moon, Third Quarter Moon, and Waning Crescent Moon, are like the first stages but in reverse, with the moon appearing smaller and smaller each time. The cycle then restarts with the New Moon.

New Words

comprise *v* be composed of	**aligned** *adj* arranged in a straight line
wane *v* get smaller	**sliver of** *n* a thin slice of
orbit around X *n* a fixed-path journey around X	**phase** *n* stage

10 minutes

Part A. Picture Description

1.

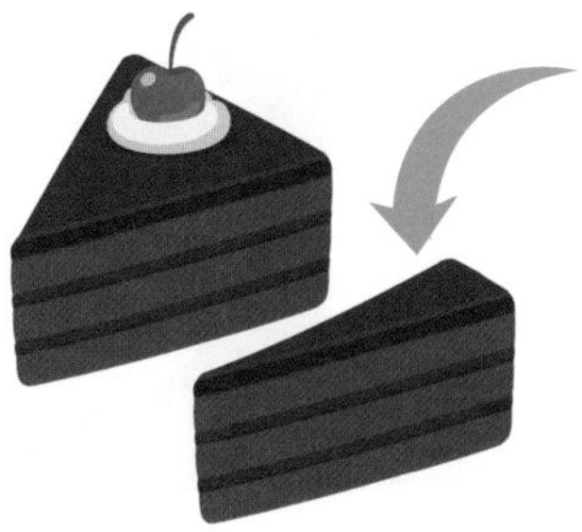

Mark said he wanted a ________ cake.

(A) whole
(B) sliver of
(C) giant piece of
(D) cherry-topped

2.

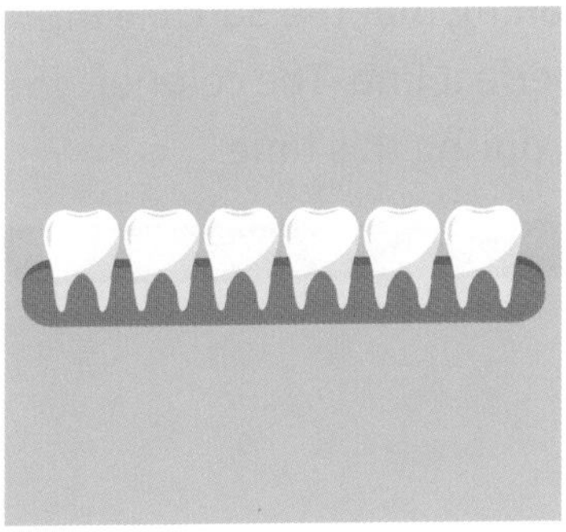

The teeth are ________.

(A) aligned
(B) reversed
(C) yellowed
(D) damaged

Part B. Sentence Completion

3. My friend Ben can recite the alphabet ________ reverse, from Z-A.

(A) in
(B) to
(C) as
(D) for

4. The satellite ________ a full orbit around the earth.

(A) is now complete
(B) is now completed
(C) has now complete
(D) has now completed

Supermoon:

The Moon appears particularly large because it is both close to Earth and is a full moon.

Blood Moon:

The Moon is in a total lunar eclipse, meaning that the Sun, Earth, and Moon are in a perfect line or near-perfect line. The color of the moon appears to be reddish-brown during this time.

Blue Moon: The second full moon in a month that has two.

Pink Moon: The first full moon in April.

Strawberry Moon: The first full moon in June, when strawberry season starts in North America.

5. When is there alignment between the Sun, Earth, and Moon?

(A) in a supermoon
(B) in a blood moon
(C) in a blue moon
(D) in a strawberry moon

6. What is true about a blue moon?

(A) There is a lunar eclipse.
(B) There is a signal that spring is starting.
(C) There is more than one full moon in a month.
(D) There is more grayish-blue color in the moon than usual.

Part D. General Reading Comprehension

Every 29.53 days (a lunar month), the moon goes through a cycle of darkness, light, and different shapes to the human eye. We call this the waxing (getting bigger) and waning (getting smaller) of the moon.

In western cultures, waxing and waning comprises eight phases. In the first phase, the moon appears completely dark to those of us on Earth as the sun and moon are aligned. This is called the New Moon. The next phase is the Waxing Crescent Moon, where we can start to see a little sliver of the moon. The sliver keeps growing and reaches the First Quarter Moon, the phase in which the moon has now completed a fourth of its orbit around the earth. At the First Quarter, the moon looks like a perfect half-circle from Earth. The Waxing Gibbous Moon phase comes next. "Gibbous" refers to the specific shape of the moon here — bigger than a semi-circle, but not yet a full circle. Finally, the moon gets to the Full Moon, where the moon looks like a full circle.

The other phases, called Waning Gibbous Moon, Third Quarter Moon, and Waning Crescent Moon, are like the first stages but in reverse, with the moon appearing smaller and smaller each time. The cycle then restarts with the New Moon.

7. What would be the best title for the passage?
   (A) Rabbit in the Moon
   (B) Moon-related Holidays
   (C) The Moon's Eight Phases
   (D) The Many Moons of Jupiter

8. What happens during the New Moon?
   (A) The moon attracts wolves.
   (B) The moon is at its brightest.
   (C) The moon looks like a crescent.
   (D) The moon looks dark from Earth.

9. When does the moon look like a perfect half-circle from Earth?
   (A) when it is in its eighth phase
   (B) when it has completed a quarter of its earthly orbit
   (C) when it is waning after the Waning Crescent Moon
   (D) when it is one day after the Waxing Gibbous phase

10. What does "Waxing Gibbous" mean?
   (A) bigger than a semi-circle, and growing
   (B) smaller than a semi-circle, and growing
   (C) bigger than a semi-circle, and shrinking
   (D) smaller than a semi-circle, and shrinking

Listening Practice

Listen and write.

MP3 HJ2-10

Phases of the Moon

Every 29.53 days (a lunar month), the moon goes through a cycle of darkness, light, and different shapes to the human eye. We call this the waxing (getting bigger) and [1] ________ (getting smaller) of the moon.

In western cultures, waxing and waning [2] ________ eight phases. In the first phase, the moon appears completely dark to those of us on Earth as the sun and moon are [3] ________. This is called the New Moon. The next phase is the Waxing Crescent Moon, where we can start to see a little [4] ________ of the moon. The sliver keeps growing and reaches the First Quarter Moon, the phase in which the moon has now completed a fourth of its [5] ________ around the earth. At the First Quarter, the moon looks like a perfect half-circle from Earth. The Waxing Gibbous Moon phase comes next. "Gibbous" refers to the specific shape of the moon here – bigger than a semi-circle, but not yet a full circle. Finally, the moon gets to the Full Moon, where the moon looks like a full circle.

The other [6] ________, called Waning Gibbous Moon, Third Quarter Moon, and Waning Crescent Moon, are like the first stages but in reverse, with the moon appearing smaller and smaller each time. The cycle then restarts with the New Moon.

Word Bank

orbit	orbet	sliver
silver	comprises	alined
comprizes	waning	wanning
phases	aligned	fazes

Listen. Pause. Say each sentence.

MP3 HJ2-10G

Writing Practice

Write the words.

1 ________________ *v* be composed of	2 ________________ *adj* arranged in a straight line
3 ________________ *v* get smaller	4 ________________ *n* a thin slice of
5 ________________ X *n* a fixed-path journey around X	6 ________________ *n* stage

Write the words in each blank.

Summary

Every lunar month, the moon goes through a cycle of waxing and ________________. This comprises eight ________________. The moon ________________ from the New Moon, to the Waxing Crescent Moon, the First Quarter Moon, the Waxing Gibbous Moon, and finally the Full Moon. Then the moon keeps shrinking and the ________________ then restarts.

Word Puzzle

Complete the word puzzle.

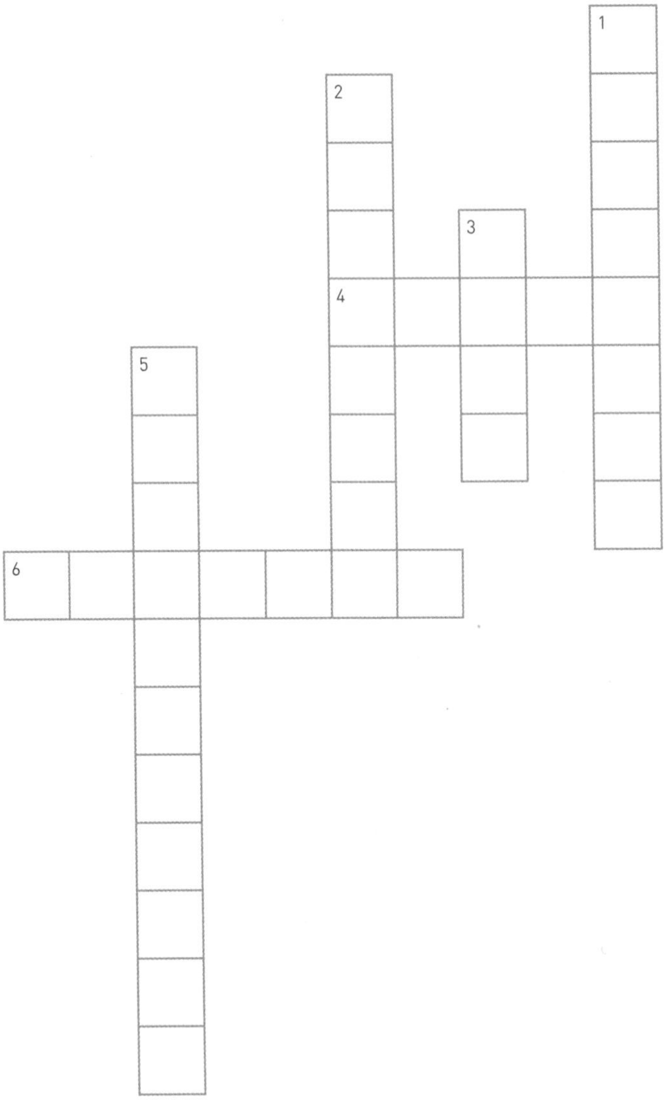

Across

4 stage

6 arranged in a straight line

Down

1 a thin slice of

2 be composed of

3 get smaller

5 a fixed-path journey around X

Teacher's Book
p.168

UNIT 11

Plasma

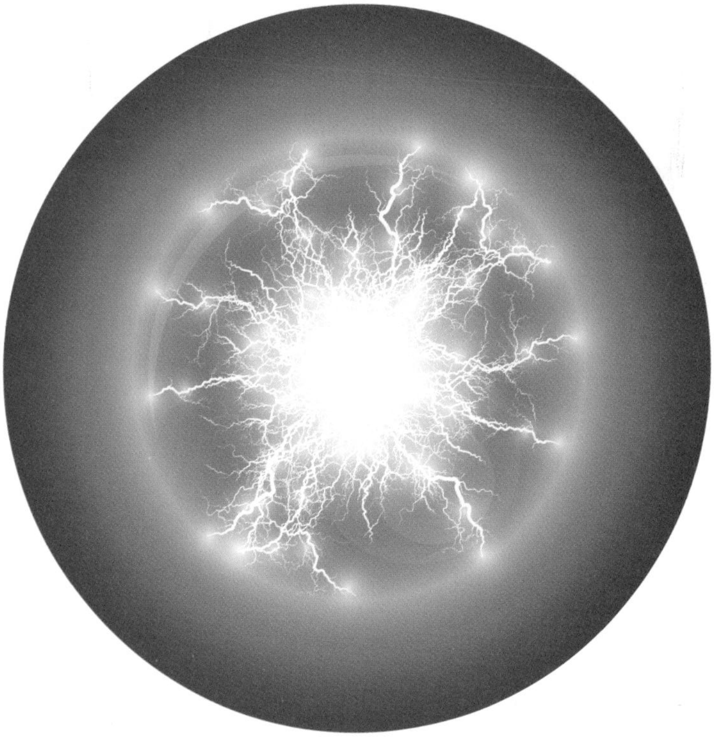

Write the missing word from this list of states of matter:
solid, ________, gas.
Is there a fourth state of matter?

UNIT 11 Plasma

People used to divide matter into three fundamental states: solids, liquids, and gases. However, there is actually a fourth state of matter. In fact, as far as we know, it is the most common state of matter in the whole observable universe. Most stars are made of it, the Sun is made of it, and even many television sets are made of it. This state of matter is a hot gas known as a plasma.

A plasma is a gas that has been pumped with energy and then sparked. When a gas becomes hot enough, some of its electrons will break free from their nucleus but will continue to travel around with the nucleus. This forms a plasma. In the case of the Sun, for example, the extreme heat causes hydrogen and helium molecules to fly off, generating a giant plasma ball.

It is thought that 99% of the observable universe is made up of plasmas, but on Earth naturally-occurring plasmas are relatively rare. There are a few places where we can see it though: in the Northern and Southern Lights and in lightning. Still, if we look up at the sky and contemplate the rest of the universe, we can remember that a lot of it is a plasma.

New Words

matter *n* physical substance	**fundamental** *adj* basic
state *n* a condition	**electron** *n* a negatively charged particle
nucleus *n* the central core of an atom, with a positive charge	**molecule** *n* a group of atoms bonded together

10 minutes

Part A. Picture Description

1.

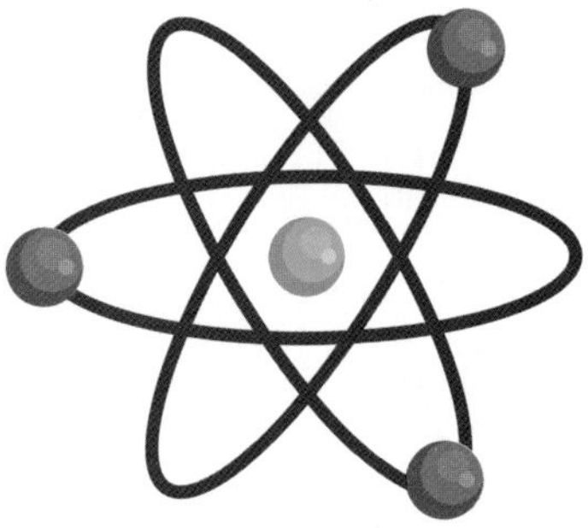

The blue circle represents the ________ of the atom.

(A) shell
(B) bomb
(C) nucleus
(D) absorption

2.

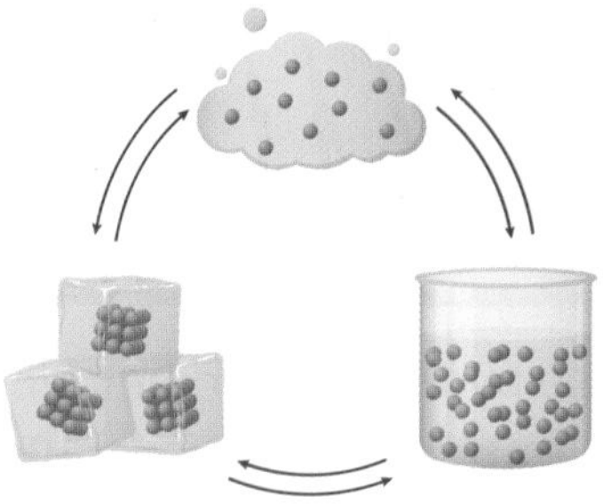

This graphic shows three different ________ of matter.

(A) states
(B) liquids
(C) gases
(D) solids

Part B. Sentence Completion

3. If you ________ up at the sky, you will see the Northern Lights.

(A) look
(B) had looked
(C) were looking
(D) could have looked

4. A plasma is a hot gas ________ with energy and then lit up.

(A) that pumps
(B) can be pumped
(C) has been pumped
(D) that has been pumped

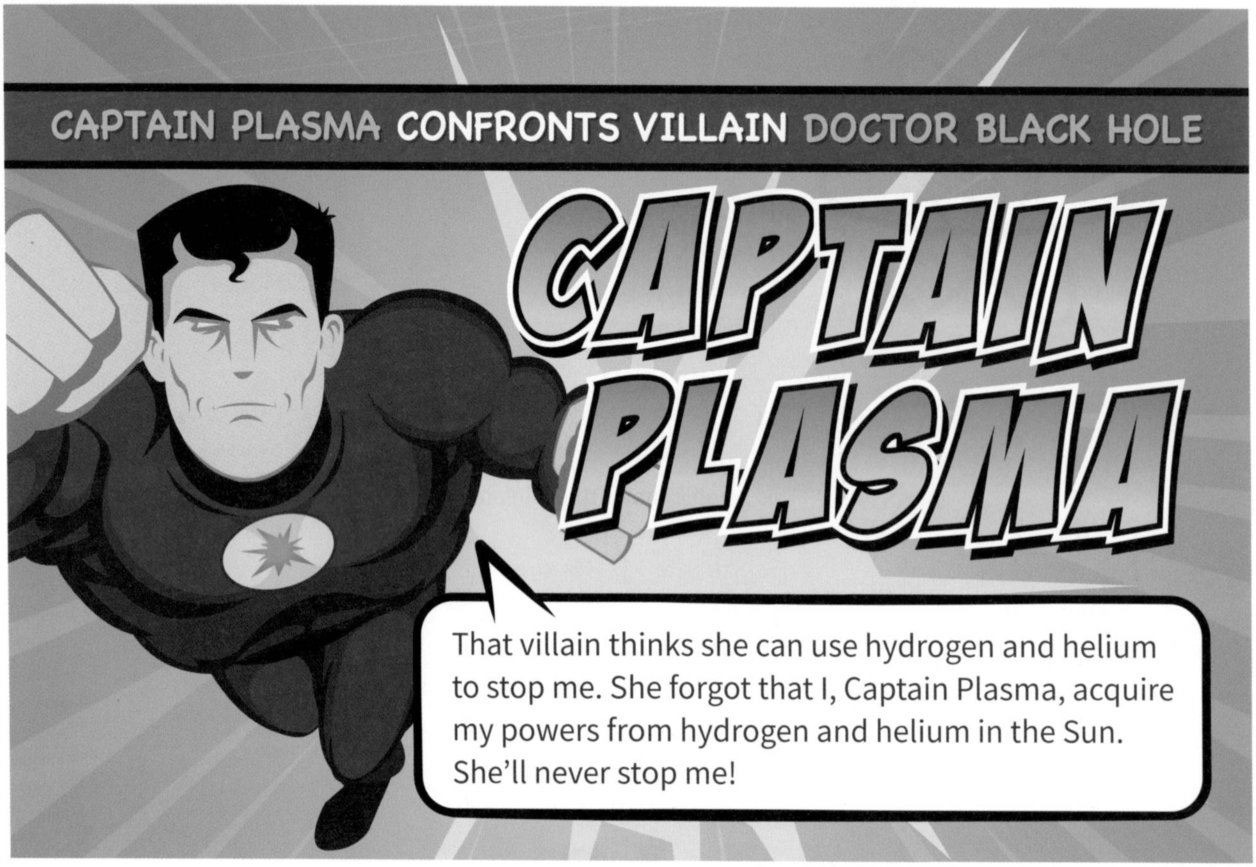

5. What can be inferred about Doctor Black Hole?

(A) She is the enemy of Captain Plasma.
(B) She gave Captain Plasma his powers.
(C) She stopped making hydrogen and helium.
(D) She created a freeze ray with the power of the Sun.

6. What is mentioned about Captain Plasma?

(A) He is the brother of Doctor Black Hole.
(B) He was born on a planet far from Earth.
(C) He returned hydrogen and helium to the Sun.
(D) He gets his powers from two elements in the Sun.

Part D. General Reading Comprehension

People used to divide matter into three fundamental states: solids, liquids, and gases. However, there is actually a fourth state of matter. In fact, as far as we know, it is the most common state of matter in the whole observable universe. Most stars are made of it, the Sun is made of it, and even many television sets are made of it. This state of matter is a hot gas known as a plasma.

A plasma is a gas that has been pumped with energy and then sparked. When a gas becomes hot enough, some of its electrons will break free from their nucleus but will continue to travel around with the nucleus. This forms a plasma. In the case of the Sun, for example, the extreme heat causes hydrogen and helium molecules to fly off, generating a giant plasma ball.

It is thought that 99% of the observable universe is made up of plasmas, but on Earth naturally-occurring plasmas are relatively rare. There are a few places where we can see it though: in the Northern and Southern Lights and in lightning. Still, if we look up at the sky and contemplate the rest of the universe, we can remember that a lot of it is a plasma.

7. What is the passage mainly about?
   (A) the fourth state of matter
   (B) the three states of matter
   (C) how atoms form the universe
   (D) how much of the universe is observable

8. Which of the following is made of a plasma?
   (A) stars
   (B) radios
   (C) the Moon
   (D) the Amazon River

9. When will electrons break free and travel with their nucleus?
   (A) when a gas gets very hot
   (B) when a liquid becomes a solid
   (C) when a gas is cooled to a liquid
   (D) when a solid touches another solid

10. What difference is listed between Earth and the rest of the observable universe?
   (A) Earth has no naturally occurring plasmas.
   (B) Earth has few naturally occurring plasmas.
   (C) Earth has hotter naturally occurring plasmas.
   (D) Earth has a lot of naturally occurring plasmas.

Listening Practice

Listen and write.

MP3 HJ2-11

Plasma

People used to divide matter into three 1 ________ states: solids, liquids, and gases. However, there is actually a fourth 2 ________ of 3 ________. In fact, as far as we know, it is the most common state of matter in the whole observable universe. Most stars are made of it, the Sun is made of it, and even many television sets are made of it. This state of matter is a hot gas known as a plasma.

A plasma is a gas that has been pumped with energy and then sparked. When a gas becomes hot enough, some of its 4 ________ will break free from their nucleus but will continue to travel around with the 5 ________. This forms a plasma. In the case of the Sun, for example, the extreme heat causes hydrogen and helium 6 ________ to fly off, generating a giant plasma ball.

It is thought that 99% of the observable universe is made up of plasmas, but on Earth naturally-occurring plasmas are relatively rare. There are a few places where we can see it though: in the Northern and Southern Lights and in lightning. Still, if we look up at the sky and contemplate the rest of the universe, we can remember that a lot of it is a plasma.

Word Bank

matter	molecules	State
state	nucleus	madder
fundemental	molecyules	electruns
fundamental	nuclius	electrons

Listen. Pause. Say each sentence.

MP3 HJ2-11G

Writing Practice

Write the words.

1 ______________ *n* physical substance	2 ______________ *adj* basic
3 ______________ *n* a condition	4 ______________ *n* a negatively charged particle
5 ______________ *n* the central core of an atom, with a positive charge	6 ______________ *n* a group of atoms bonded together

Write the words in each blank.

Summary

Plasma is the most common state of ______________ in the whole observable universe. A plasma is a gas that has been ______________ with energy and then sparked. Although naturally-occurring plasmas are relatively ______________ on Earth, we can ______________ that a lot of the universe is made of plasmas.

Word Puzzle

Complete the word puzzle.

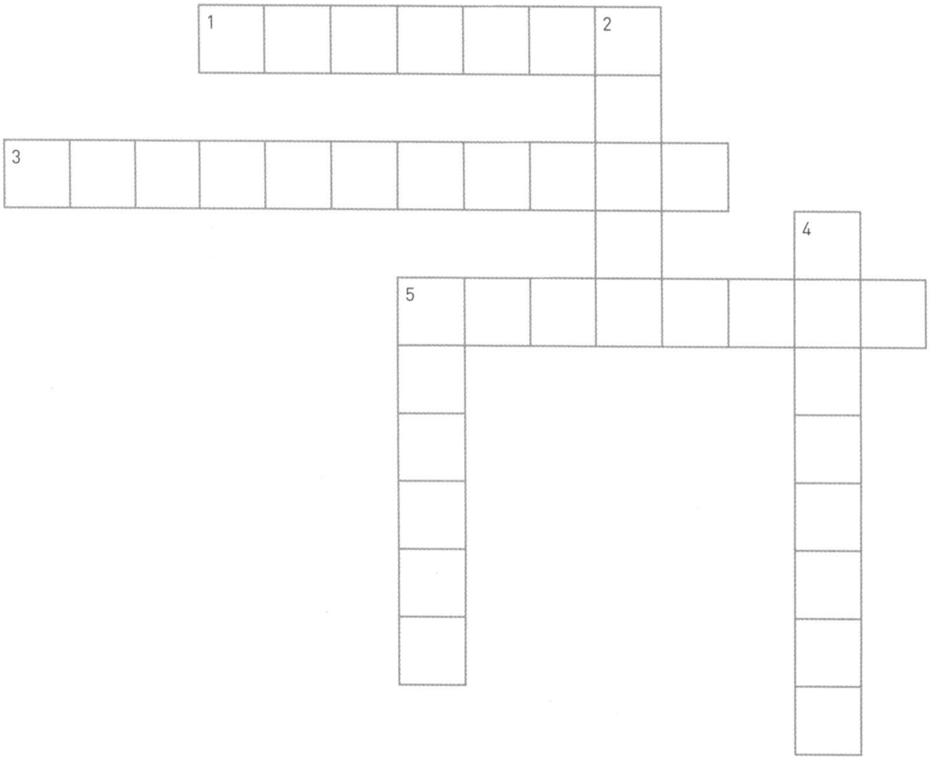

Across

1 the central core of an atom, with a positive charge

3 basic

5 a group of atoms bonded together

Down

2 a condition

4 a negatively charged particle

5 physical substance

Teacher's Book
p.173

UNIT 12

Contagious Yawning

When do you yawn?

UNIT 12 Contagious Yawning

Birds, reptiles, mammals, and some fish all yawn. Yawns are an involuntary reaction that originate in the brain stem. However, for only a few creatures, including humans, yawning is contagious. When we see another person yawn, it is six times more likely that we will also yawn. Yet scientists still do not know why this occurs.

Numerous theories have been proposed to explain the phenomenon of contagious yawning. One theory is that yawning is related to empathy, the ability to feel along with others. Support for this theory comes from observations of some children with autistic spectrum disorder, a condition that seems to affect people's ability to sense what others are feeling. When those children were watching a video of people yawning, they yawned less than children without the disorder.

However, a different theory is that contagious yawning is related to mirror neurons in the brain. These mirror neurons are thought to cause organisms to mimic behaviors, perhaps because they recognize in others a behavior that might be useful for survival.

While it is not yet known why contagious yawning happens, there is plenty of evidence that it occurs, even just from reading about it. If you yawned while reading this fascinating passage, contagious yawning is probably the reason!

New Words

yawn *v* open your mouth and breathe in when you are tired or bored	contagious *adj* spreadable to other people
involuntary *adj* without wanting to	empathy *n* the ability to understand the feelings of others
disorder *n* a problem or illness with the mind or body	mimic *v* copy

Part A. Picture Description

1.

Ramona is ________. I guess she's tired.

(A) napping
(B) yawning
(C) sleeping
(D) crawling

2.

The man in green's cold is ________.

(A) contained
(B) contagious
(C) diminishing
(D) disappearing

Part B. Sentence Completion

3. Many different theories have been ________ to explain this interesting phenomenon.

(A) propose
(B) proposal
(C) proposed
(D) proposing

4. ________ children watched a video of animals running, the children smiled more.

(A) Who
(B) When
(C) There
(D) Those

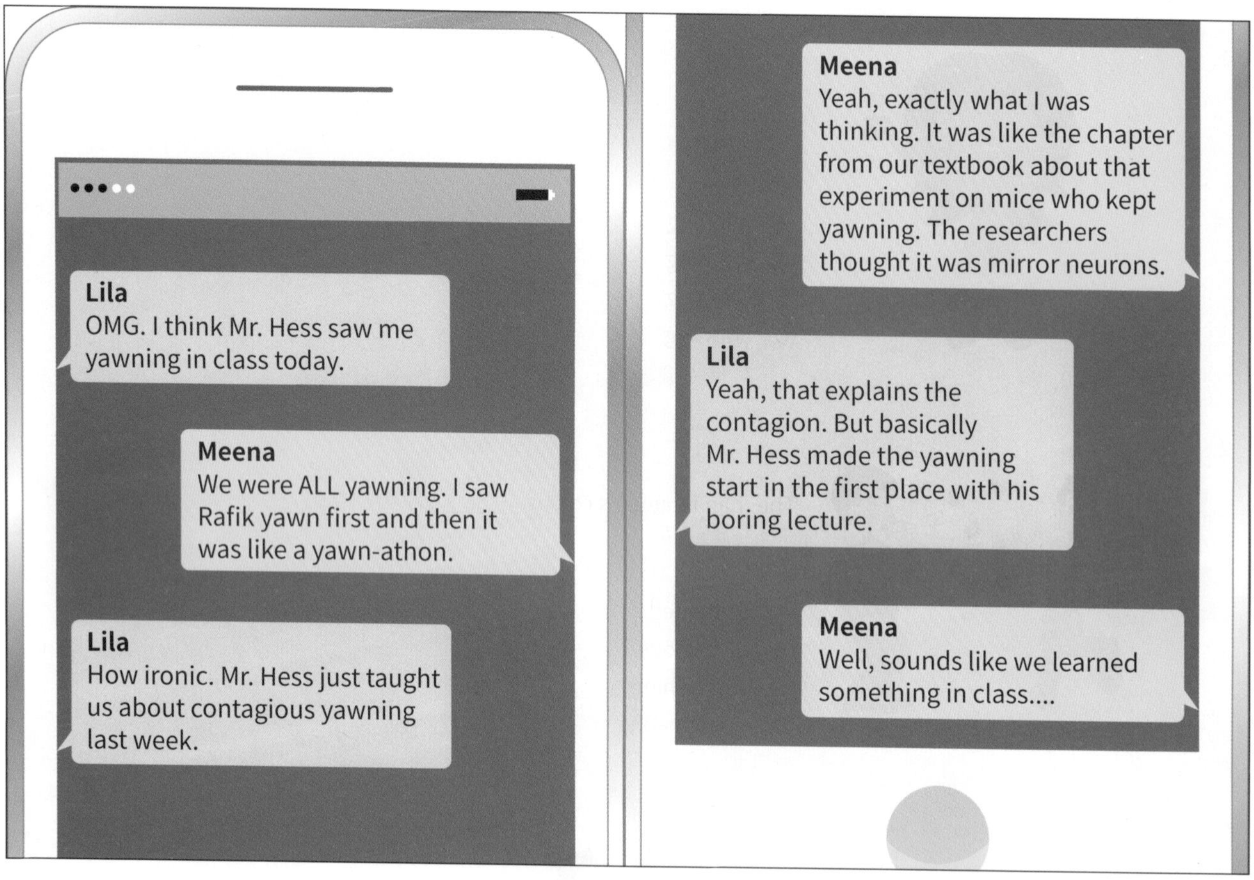

5. What subject does Mr. Hess most likely teach?

(A) biology
(B) physics
(C) mathematics
(D) computer science

6. According to Lila, what happened in class?

(A) Mr. Hess began yawning first.
(B) Mr. Hess made some mice yawn.
(C) Mr. Hess caught Rafik yawning in class.
(D) Mr. Hess started the contagious yawning.

Part D. General Reading Comprehension

Birds, reptiles, mammals, and some fish all yawn. Yawns are an involuntary reaction that originate in the brain stem. However, for only a few creatures, including humans, yawning is contagious. When we see another person yawn, it is six times more likely that we will also yawn. Yet scientists still do not know why this occurs.

Numerous theories have been proposed to explain the phenomenon of contagious yawning. One theory is that yawning is related to empathy, the ability to feel along with others. Support for this theory comes from observations of some children with autistic spectrum disorder, a condition that seems to affect people's ability to sense what others are feeling. When those children were watching a video of people yawning, they yawned less than children without the disorder.

However, a different theory is that contagious yawning is related to mirror neurons in the brain. These mirror neurons are thought to cause organisms to mimic behaviors, perhaps because they recognize in others a behavior that might be useful for survival.

While it is not yet known why contagious yawning happens, there is plenty of evidence that it occurs, even just from reading about it. If you yawned while reading this fascinating passage, contagious yawning is probably the reason!

7. What is the best title for the passage?

(A) Six Theories about Yawning
(B) Contagious Yawning in Animals
(C) The Importance of Hiding Yawns
(D) The Mystery of Contagious Yawning

8. According to the passage, what happened when some children with a disorder watched a video?

(A) They stood up when yawning.
(B) They stopped yawning forever.
(C) They yawned more than a control group.
(D) They yawned less than children without the disorder.

9. According to one theory, what might cause mimicking in yawning?

(A) mirror neurons
(B) the brain stem
(C) scientific observations
(D) autistic spectrum disorder

10. According to the passage, what can trigger contagious yawning?

(A) seeing a bird
(B) reading about it
(C) going swimming
(D) looking at a light

Listening Practice

Listen and write.

MP3 HJ2-12

Contagious Yawning

Birds, reptiles, mammals, and some fish all [1] ______________. Yawns are an [2] ______________ reaction that originate in the brain stem. However, for only a few creatures, including humans, yawning is contagious. When we see another person yawn, it is six times more likely that we will also yawn. Yet scientists still do not know why this occurs.

Numerous theories have been proposed to explain the phenomenon of [3] ______________ yawning. One theory is that yawning is related to [4] ______________, the ability to feel along with others. Support for this theory comes from observations of some children with autistic spectrum [5] ______________, a condition that seems to affect people's ability to sense what others are feeling. When those children were watching a video of people yawning, they yawned less than children without the disorder.

However, a different theory is that contagious yawning is related to mirror neurons in the brain. These mirror neurons are thought to cause organisms to [6] ______________ behaviors, perhaps because they recognize in others a behavior that might be useful for survival.

While it is not yet known why contagious yawning happens, there is plenty of evidence that it occurs, even just from reading about it. If you yawned while reading this fascinating passage, contagious yawning is probably the reason!

Word Bank

mimic	empathy	disorder
contagous	yawns	this order
yawn	involuntery	enpathy
mimmic	contagious	involuntary

Listen. Pause. Say each sentence.

MP3 HJ2-12G

Writing Practice

Write the words.

1 ____________ *v* open your mouth and breathe in when you are tired or bored	2 ____________ *adj* spreadable to other people
3 ____________ *adj* without wanting to	4 ____________ *n* the ability to understand the feelings of others
5 ____________ *n* a problem or illness with the mind or body	6 ____________ *v* copy

Write the words in each blank.

Summary

For a few creatures including humans, yawning is ____________. There are several theories proposed to explain this ____________. One theory is related to empathy, and another is related to mirror ____________ in the brain. While it is not yet known why contagious ____________ happens, there is plenty of evidence that it occurs.

Word Puzzle

Complete the word puzzle.

Across

1 copy

3 a problem or illness with the mind or body

4 spreadable to other people

5 the ability to understand the feelings of others

6 open your mouth and breathe in when you are tired or bored

Down

2 without wanting to

AMAZING STORIES

The Unsolved Mystery of Planet Nine

Teacher's Book p.179

In the outer regions of our Solar System there is a mysterious group of objects orbiting the Sun. Some of them go around the planet Neptune, pulled into its orbit by gravity. But some of the objects are being pulled away from Neptune into another orbit. Something must be there in space pulling the objects away. That something must be very big, with an even greater mass than Neptune. That something could be Planet Nine.

We do not actually know for sure if Planet Nine exists. At the moment, it is considered a hypothetical planet. But in 2014, scientists began to theorize that something in space must be controlling the orbit of these objects. If there is a planet there, scientists believe that it is even bigger than Earth, with five to ten times the mass of our home planet. One theory is that Planet Nine is the core of a huge planet whose orbit began when the Solar System was formed. Another theory is that the planet came from somewhere else and was pulled into our Solar System by a star that was passing by.

However, no one has been able to find Planet Nine yet. If Planet Nine exists, its orbit around the Sun would be 400 to 800 times the distance of Earth's orbit. Modern telescopes cannot see anything there because the light reflected on the planet from the Sun is not bright enough. It is hoped that a combination of computer simulations and better telescopes will help astronomers to solve the mystery of Planet Nine.

ANSWERS

CHAPTER 1 | Health
p.10

UNIT 1
HJ2-1
p.11

1 (C) 2 (B) 3 (B) 4 (B) 5 (C) 6 (A) 7 (B) 8 (C) 9 (B) 10 (A)
1 scenario 2 diabetes 3 relieved 4 literacy 5 societal 6 providers
1 scenario 2 diabetes 3 relieved 4 literacy 5 societal 6 health care providers
literacy, recognition, government, low
→ 4 scenario 5 diabetes ↓ 1 literacy 2 health care providers 3 relieved 4 societal

UNIT 2
HJ2-2
p.19

1 (C) 2 (A) 3 (A) 4 (A) 5 (C) 6 (A) 7 (B) 8 (A) 9 (D) 10 (A)
1 Virtually 2 metabolism 3 cardiovascular 4 significant 5 traumatic 6 enhance
1 virtually everyone 2 metabolism 3 cardiovascular 4 statistically significant 5 traumatic 6 enhance
both, mental, muscle, enhance
→ 6 virtually everyone ↓ 1 statistically significant 2 cardiovascular 3 enhance 4 traumatic 5 metabolism

UNIT 3
HJ2-3
p.27

1 (A) 2 (B) 3 (C) 4 (A) 5 (C) 6 (D) 7 (A) 8 (D) 9 (A) 10 (B)
1 strain 2 eyewear 3 blinking 4 combat 5 humidifier 6 modified
1 strain 2 eyewear 3 blink 4 combat 5 humidifier 6 modify
blue light, mobile, fake, combat
→ 5 modify 6 strain ↓ 1 combat 2 humidifier 3 blink 4 eyewear

UNIT 4
HJ2-4
p.35

1 (C) 2 (B) 3 (A) 4 (C) 5 (D) 6 (B) 7 (C) 8 (C) 9 (C) 10 (C)
1 diet 2 apocalypse 3 nutritionists 4 fiber 5 appetite 6 starvation
1 diet 2 apocalypse 3 nutritionist 4 fiber 5 appetite 6 starvation
diet, white, nutrients, bored
→ 4 starvation 6 apocalypse ↓ 1 fiber 2 nutritionist 3 diet 5 appetite

CHAPTER 2 | Environment
p.44

UNIT 5
HJ2-5
p.45

1 (B) 2 (B) 3 (B) 4 (B) 5 (C) 6 (D) 7 (A) 8 (B) 9 (A) 10 (D)
1 underway 2 documented 3 invasive 4 ticks 5 droughts 6 drastic
1 underway 2 documented 3 invasive species 4 tick 5 drought 6 drastic
underway, occur, take, effects
→ 1 tick 3 drastic 4 underway 5 documented ↓ 2 invasive species 5 drought

UNIT 6
HJ2-6
p.53

1 (A) 2 (C) 3 (C) 4 (A) 5 (B) 6 (B) 7 (C) 8 (C) 9 (D) 10 (C)
1 prompted 2 retailers 3 Proponents 4 claim 5 fuels 6 adjusted
1 prompt 2 retailer 3 proponent 4 claim 5 fossil fuel 6 adjust
explored, delivery, alternative, saves
→ 4 fossil fuel 5 prompt ↓ 1 retailer 2 adjust 3 claim 5 proponent

UNIT 7
HJ2-7
p.61

1 (A) 2 (B) 3 (A) 4 (B) 5 (D) 6 (A) 7 (D) 8 (D) 9 (A) 10 (D)
1 goose 2 evolved 3 declined 4 Estimates 5 endangered 6 suggest
1 goose 2 evolve 3 decline 4 estimate 5 endangered 6 suggest
endangered, zoologists, save, taken
→ 5 endangered 6 evolve ↓ 1 estimate 2 goose 3 suggest 4 decline

UNIT 8
HJ2-8
p.69

1 (C) 2 (D) 3 (B) 4 (C) 5 (C) 6 (C) 7 (D) 8 (B) 9 (C) 10 (C)
1 winding 2 body of water 3 continents 4 broke away 5 Eventually 6 flow
1 winding 2 body of water 3 continent 4 break away 5 flow 6 eventually
drastically, flow, formed, direction
→ 1 body of water 4 winding 5 flow ↓ 1 break away 2 eventually 3 continent

CHAPTER 3 | Science
p.78

UNIT 9
HJ2-9
p.79

1 (C) 2 (C) 3 (B) 4 (A) 5 (C) 6 (B) 7 (B) 8 (D) 9 (A) 10 (B)
1 broadly 2 neurons 3 implicit 4 explicit 5 clump 6 activated
1 broadly 2 neuron 3 implicit 4 explicit 5 clump 6 activate
long-term, create, accessed, activated
→ 2 broadly 4 implicit 5 clump 6 neuron ↓ 1 explicit 3 activate

UNIT 10
HJ2-10
p.87

1 (B) 2 (A) 3 (A) 4 (D) 5 (B) 6 (C) 7 (C) 8 (D) 9 (B) 10 (A)
1 waning 2 comprises 3 aligned 4 sliver 5 orbit 6 phases
1 comprise 2 aligned 3 wane 4 sliver of 5 orbit around 6 phase
waning, phases, grows, cycle
→ 4 phase 6 aligned ↓ 1 sliver of 2 comprise 3 wane 5 orbit around

UNIT 11
HJ2-11
p.95

1 (C) 2 (A) 3 (A) 4 (D) 5 (A) 6 (D) 7 (A) 8 (A) 9 (A) 10 (B)
1 fundamental 2 state 3 matter 4 electrons 5 nucleus 6 molecules
1 matter 2 fundamental 3 state 4 electron 5 nucleus 6 molecule
matter, pumped, rare, contemplate
→ 1 nucleus 3 fundamental 5 molecule ↓ 2 state 4 electron 5 matter

UNIT 12
HJ2-12
p.103

1 (B) 2 (B) 3 (C) 4 (B) 5 (A) 6 (D) 7 (D) 8 (D) 9 (A) 10 (B)
1 yawn 2 involuntary 3 contagious 4 empathy 5 disorder 6 mimic
1 yawn 2 contagious 3 involuntary 4 empathy 5 disorder 6 mimic
contagious, phenomenon, neurons, yawning
→ 1 mimic 3 disorder 4 contagious 5 empathy 6 yawn ↓ 2 involuntary